Judy Jackson

A FEAST IN FIFTEEN STORIES

A new start for hesitant cooks

Marsons

Judy Jackson worked as a translator before starting a small catering business. She then gave cookery courses, developing new ideas which later appeared in her first book, The Home Book of Jewish Cookery (Faber). A successful series in the Sunday Times led to the publication of a second book, Microwave Vegetable Cooking (Macdonald). She has contributed food articles to many national newspapers including The Telegraph, The Times, The Financial Times and the Evening Standard. Judy Jackson lives in London with her husband and the youngest of her four sons.

Marsons
101 Hamilton Terrace
London NW8 9QX

Published in London by Marsons, 1995

ISBN 0 951722018

Typeset in Monotype Bembo and Gill Sans 13/15
Typography by Adam Jackson
Cover photograph by Carl Warner
Cover design by Akio Morishima
Tablecloth and plates kindly loaned by Habitat
Printed by Dacosta Print

For Michael and David
the two men in my life who don't cook
(and for Daniel and Tim, who do)

Contents

Contents

Introduction

Mrs. Beeton was a young woman when she wrote her famous book. She knew how cooks should organise their lives. "Good work is almost impossible without early rising and punctuality" she began. Her advice ranged from wearing short dresses and well-fitting boots to gathering greens early from the garden to make "an easy task of getting rid of caterpillars." Her standards were high. "The cleaning of the kitchen passages must always be over before breakfast. A dirty kitchen is a disgrace to all concerned."

Of course, cooking in those days was a full time occupation. Modern cooks don't start to think about meals at 6 am. You are more likely to stagger home exhausted at 6 pm and then wonder what to make. Far from considering whether the kitchen is disgracefully dirty, you probably have to begin by tidying up the morning's mail or newspapers, or tripping over a few toys and unloading the shopping on to the clearest patch of work surface. The preparation of dinner can then begin.

But before you start, you need the inclination to go into the kitchen. Don't be surprised if, in spite of leafing through yet another cookery book, your enthusiasm is low. Hundreds of glossy books are published each year and food articles take up more and more space in weekend newspapers. Yet many nervous cooks are happy to read about food but reluctant to try out the recipes.

A whole generation has been put off cooking for various reasons. First there was the decade of nouvelle cuisine. The immaculate arrangements on huge plates triggered a decline in confidence. Then, as packaged food became readily available and more attractive, it hardly seemed worth the trouble trying to cook at home. Finally, working men and women simply don't have the time.

Yet there are good reasons to decide that you want to learn to cook better. It's one thing to live on ready-prepared food during the week but much harder to look your Saturday night dinner guests in the eye and tell them where you bought the marvellous pâté.

You should forget about trying to become a professional overnight and concentrate on what matters – putting together fresh and appealing food that tastes good. Once you stop worrying, you'll realise that cooking is relaxing and a good way to spend your time.

To get to this stage a new approach is needed. An adult who is learning the piano would rather play Mozart than children's tunes. It's the same with cookery. No-one wants to start by boiling an egg. Beginners are usually advised to read the whole recipe through before starting, as if a nasty surprise is awaiting them. The inexperienced cook is often told that a soufflé needs great skill. This is so discouraging. If you're learning Monopoly, you want to stop reading the rules and get on with the game.

This book is not a comprehensive cookery course. It's an exploration of how to enjoy making good food, so it starts with what can be achieved in five minutes. The first recipe can be made while you think what to do next. The next one is a starter for two and before you know it, you are making a choice of two main courses for four. Each dish takes no longer than minutes to prepare. There's no measuring, no weighing – just cooking.

The recipes are designed to give you confidence. They tell you what containers you need, when to turn on the oven and what to expect half way through. They are not graded according to difficulty because I don't think it's any harder to make a chocolate soufflé or a loaf of bread than to fry an aubergine or roast a chicken.

It doesn't need great expertise to produce the type of food most people want to eat and serve at home. That's why I am not including instructions for making spun sugar or icing wedding cakes. (The fact that I can't do either would make this difficult, too.) Nor do I want to emulate old-fashioned restaurant cooking with perfectly turned vegetables and sauces that call for a demi-glace, veal stock and a pint of cream. A successful dish today, whether at home or in a restaurant, depends on starting with bright and fresh produce, not overcooking it and presenting it in a way that makes it look good.

The chapters have themes about different aspects of food and eating. Each one also covers some new techniques so you will progress from cutting vegetables and simple stir-frying to making stocks, pancakes, pastry and cakes. Most of the basic skills you need to know are covered in the first half of the book and they are explained in the recipes that make up the menus.

I had never cooked at all before I was about seventeen and only began seriously after I married. Working as a part-time translator I soon discovered that the days spent cooking were far more fun than the hours devoted to poring over dictionaries. A few years later, with three small sons and little chance for long periods of intellectual concentration, I began a catering business from home.

Of course those years were far from trouble-free. There were disasters and moments of panic which now make me ashamed and amused. I've included some of the worst calamities because it's encouraging to read about other people's mistakes.

One of the hardest things to cope with when you are inexperienced is the pressure to entertain and to do it with style. Recipes in magazines are so often labelled "impressive". I remember trying out a dessert which called for a paper-thin chocolate wrapping. The melted chocolate had to be cooled in the freezer on a strip of foil and then left for a few crucial minutes in a warm kitchen so that it would bend into a wide ribbon. After several failed attempts and hours of work the result was impressive enough, but was it worth the tension?

Entertaining books usually feature meticulous countdowns but it would be far better to choose a menu that suits your own personality. For example you may be happy inviting guests into the kitchen to have a drink while you grill the fish and wash the salad. Or you may prefer to choose a casserole which bubbles away gently in the oven leaving you free to relax in another room till everyone is ready to eat.

There is, however, one thing which can make a drastic improvement to your approach to cooking: the much-maligned microwave oven. The big box that is probably sitting in a corner of the kitchen is one of the most useful tools you have. Everyone knows you can use a microwave to reheat a frozen dinner. Everyone thinks you can cook a jacket potato in one. The first assumption is right; the second one is wrong. The potato will certainly be soft after a few minutes, but it will also be soggy and damp.

Using the microwave properly can transform the way you've cooked before. If you read the chapters on how to master the microwave you will find out what it can and can't do. An exciting discovery is how it can melt chocolate, poach fish and steam asparagus. It works wonders on porridge, toasted almonds, stewed apple and french beans. Sticky toffee pudding and old-fashioned creamed rice can be made in minutes. Not only is cooking made simpler, you'll spend less time washing up and less money on other equipment.

Choosing the microwave to speed up parts of a recipe simplifies some of the tasks. But good cooking can never be rushed, and how to find time to devote to it is the question that still remains. A surprisingly wide range of techniques can be learned by setting aside a couple of hours each week. The best time for this is not in the evenings when there is pressure to get a meal on the table, but perhaps at the weekends. Although cooking needs practice, a more realistic goal might be to start with the occasional half hour. In this way you will still produce some good meals.

Mrs. Beeton had tremendous expertise. She described how to revive black lace with tea and included recipes for kangaroo tail soup and rabbit in aspic jelly. At the end of her book she gave advice which ranged from "Chimney, on Fire", to "Feet, tired". Today's worries are more likely to include "Clamped cars, how to cope with", "Videos, how to set" and "Salmonella, how to avoid".

Cooking should not be a burden. If you really want to learn to cook well and to do it fast, you will succeed. You can make a start by working through some of the short recipes that appeal to you. This should give you enough confidence to persevere with some of the longer ones, so that at the end you should be skilled enough to invite anyone you know to a marvellous meal. I'd count myself lucky to be one of the guests.

How to Get Started

Don't believe everything you've been told about cooking: that it's complicated, takes time and needs a lot of equipment. Entertaining your friends need not involve serving impressive dishes. You can make a good meal in half an hour, without a 'batterie de cuisine'. But to do anything well, you need to acquire some skills.

The techniques of cookery in Mrs. Beeton's time revolved around six basic methods: grilling, roasting, baking, boiling, stewing and frying. These are simply ways of describing how to apply the heat. It can come from above or below (grilling or frying) or it can circulate round the food. In an oven the heat is dry and this is what's called roasting or baking. Actually immersing the food in hot liquid – water, stock or fat – is what happens when you boil, stew or fry.

Although the methods have changed very little, the equipment used today is vastly different, making a much simpler task of turning a pile of raw ingredients into a cooked dish. Non-stick pans, blenders and electric whisks have transformed the way people cook. The microwave, often dismissed as a method of heating and defrosting, is the perfect way to apply moist heat.

If the tedious preparation can be minimised, that leaves more time to spend on the happy part and that includes reading about what to make. You are about to take a leap into the deep end – no testing the water with a choice of Starters, Main Courses and Desserts. You are going to attempt a complete meal, starting in reverse order with something to munch with your coffee. Each chapter has a menu with recipes that feature several new techniques, which gradually build up an understanding of how different foods are cooked. The quantities serve four people, unless otherwise stated.

Mastering each task is not hard, but putting them together to produce a whole meal can be more daunting. With more experience you will learn how to slice aubergines while the onions are frying or how to buzz up some mayonnaise while the potatoes are boiling. It may be a surprise to discover that making a cooked breakfast like scrambled eggs on toast with mushrooms requires more skill and co-ordination than any of the recipes in the 'just-back-from-shopping' menu in Chapter 2.

The more complicated processes, like rolling pastry or turning out pancakes, need a little practice to get good results. But to produce a delicate soup, a perfectly risen soufflé or a pile of chocolate leaves could well be far easier than you imagine. Enough comments. Why not begin now?

The Menu

Almond, Onion and Mushroom Pâté

• • •

Stir–Fried Steak with Vegetables

Roast Rack of Lamb

Bulghur Pilaff

Salad

• • •

Chocolate Apricots

The Techniques

Melting chocolate

Stir–frying

Roasting

Steaming

Five Minutes in the Kitchen

A doctor, after examining a patient, told him gently that he only had a short time to live. "How long?" asked the patient. The doctor hesitated and then said: "About five minutes, actually".

"Can't you do anything for me, doctor?" pleaded the man.

"How about a poached egg on toast?" came the reply.

It's obvious from the joke that the poor patient was dealing with someone who didn't specialise in cooking. Experts would have you believe that a beginner should start with a boiled egg, but there are more exciting dishes that take as little as five minutes. Choosing what to cook needs some thought and since it's easier to think while you're eating, here is something to munch while you consider the next move.

Chocolate Apricots

some dried apricots
a bar of plain chocolate

You will need: a small saucepan; a china or glass bowl that will stand over it; a sheet of tin foil and a spoon.

Open a packet of dried apricots – the kind that have been presoaked so that they are soft enough to eat in handfuls straight from the pack. Break half a bar (about 3oz or 75g) of plain dark chocolate into the bowl. Put some hot water into the saucepan and bring it to the boil. Now comes the moment when you start to exercise your skill: lower the bowl into the saucepan so it is standing just above the boiling water. Turn the heat down until it is just simmering and wait for a minute or two until the chocolate starts to melt. This is not hard – but just make sure that the water doesn't boil over into the chocolate, otherwise it spoils.

Snip about 8 apricots into strips and arrange a piece of foil on a large plate. Stir the melted chocolate with the spoon and lift the hot bowl off the saucepan. Dip one end of each apricot strip into the melted chocolate and arrange them on the foil. Put the plate into the fridge to harden the chocolate. After a short time you can peel the apricot strips off the foil. They keep well in the fridge or freezer and are good served with black coffee after dinner. Alternatively take them out and eat a few while you contemplate what to make next.

I began to think seriously about what can be made in five minutes after an embarrassing moment on live radio. The producers of programmes on small radio stations need to fill many hours in between the music and advertisements. They sometimes invite authors to talk about their books. In return for the free publicity, the writers are expected to deal with impromptu questions from the public.

I once accepted an invitation to speak about cooking on an obscure frequency that no-one could ever find. The phone-in began. I sat with headphones opposite the interviewer and although I could talk to the callers, he had a head start in vetting the questions first to see that no-one said anything rude. The questions came fast:

"What do you serve to a vegetarian who doesn't like vegetables?" "Is it safe to put foreign coins in a Christmas pudding or does it have to be an old sixpence?"

After the calls I was expected to give some encouraging advice and recipes. The interviewer started brightly: "Now Judy, the average working woman spends six and a half minutes getting dinner on the table. What do you suggest for tonight?" Thinking fast, the only thing that came to mind was a quotation from a Chinese newspaper: "Take one cockroach, marinate in wine for a day, fry in beef fat and smother with chocolate." Since that humiliating occasion, I have thought of a far better dish – a quick and stylish mushroom pâté.

The combination of speed and haute cuisine is not that new. An eccentric cook called Edward de Pomiane wrote a book called "Cooking in Ten Minutes". He relied heavily on the technique of boiling and suggested that the first thing you should do when you come home is to put a pan of water to boil before you even take your coat off.

Someone who is new to cooking will find it far more satisfying to grill or fry which is what you will do in the next recipe. The sizzle of meat or vegetables browned over direct heat is more appetising than the steam rising from a soggy cauliflower.

The recipe for stir–fried steak takes, strictly speaking, two lots of five minutes. The first five are preparation and can be done at any time. The method is called frying in English, sautéeing in French and cooking in a wok in Chinese. The principle is the same: using a large open pan, very little oil, and stirring the food briefly over intense heatto cook and br own it quickly. Nothing can go wrong. Whereas butter burns at a fairly low temperature, oil needs to be a lot hotter so it won't burn if you stir and watch the food. When the cooking is finished you should serve it straight away because most fried food is a disaster when it is limp and cool.

An American food magazine called Gourmet was famous for recipes with obscure ingredients and no short cuts. One issue contained what must be the most ridiculous lunch recipe ever invented. The title was something like: "United Nations Eggs".

These were the instructions: "Boil some Jerusalem artichokes and remove the hot centres. Wash and cook some spinach. Make a 'roux' and then a bechamel sauce. Make a separate hollandaise sauce. Toast 4 English muffins. Poach 4 eggs." It continued: "Arrange the spinach on the muffins and spoon over the white sauce. Top each one with an artichoke bottom, cover with a poached egg. Pour over the hollandaise sauce and brown under the grill."

This dish requires five saucepans and a grill pan and preferably three chefs to have everything ready at the right moment. To do it single-handed would involve keeping an eye on the toaster while you poach the eggs with one hand and whisk the tricky sauce with the other.

With far less trouble, you could serve four people with a generous and welcoming meal. Even more important, there would be less washing up in the sink and no worries about getting everything together at the right moment. The last recipe in this chapter is really three dishes in one. Each part takes about five minutes to prepare.

Life today is complicated enough without making food a big concern. Real worries are about finding jobs or coping with HP payments. Imagined ones are whether your children will ever come out of nappies (by which time they may be crashing the car and bringing home unspeakable friends). It's bad enough moving house or dealing with builders, without agonising over dinner.

If you didn't believe it possible to make a sucessful meal in minutes, here's a chance to give it a try.

Almond, Onion and Mushroom Pâté

A dip or a small starter for two.

an onion
some butter
about six mushrooms
some parsley
about half a cup of ground almond

You will need: a small frying pan.

Cut a medium-sized onion in half and with a sharp knife, chop it into small pieces. (The best way to do this is to cut slices and then, holding these together, turn the onion round and cut it in the other direction.) Wash and dry the mushrooms and a small bunch of parsley. Cut the mushrooms into small pieces and chop the parsley finely, discarding the tough stems.

Put a knob of salted butter (about a teaspoonful) in a frying pan. Turn the heat to high, toss in the chopped onion and stir for a minute or two until the onion starts to colour slightly. Turn the heat down to stop the butter burning and then add the chopped mushrooms to the pan. Keep stirring while the vegetables continue to fry. When the juices from the mushrooms start to run, you can turn the heat up again, sprinkle over some salt and pepper and throw in the parsley. Then stir in enough ground almond to make the mixture spoonable (about half a cup) and turn off the heat.

The pâté is now ready but tastes better cold. It goes well with thin toast or sticks of raw vegetables. If you don't like chunky bits, use a food processor for half a minute to get a smooth texture. You can serve it spooned on to plates or in small individual pots.

Stir–Fried Steak with Vegetables

This is a single-pan dish which will serve two people. Freezing the steak for a short time makes it easier to slice.

a carrot
a courgette
some fat spring onions
a leek
a handful beansprouts, sugar peas or mangetout
a tender steak (about half a pound)
a few tablespoons of oil
good soy sauce

You will need: a sharp knife and a very large non-stick frying pan or a wok.

Wash and dry the vegetables. Slice the carrots, courgette and leeks diagonally so that you get fairly thin large oval slices. Cut the steak into thin strips. Have ready two warmed plates.

When you are ready to start the cooking heat a few tablespoons of oil in a wok or large non-stick frying pan. It takes less than a minute and is ready when a slice of vegetable sizzles as it hits the pan. Starting with the hardest vegetables, (the carrot, onion, leek or courgette) throw the slices into the oil, tossing them over high heat for a minute or two. When they start to brown, move them to one side, add a little more oil if necessary and slide in the slices of steak. Keep the heat high and stir fry the meat for one or two minutes. It will cook very quickly and as soon as each side is no longer red, lift it with a spoon on to the cooked vegetables. Add the mangetout, sugar peas or beansprouts to the space left in the pan and toss these for a minute. Sprinkle over some pepper and a little salt. Don't overseason because it is easier to add more at the table than to save a dish which is oversalted. Pile the steak and vegetables on to the two heated plates and serve with a sprinkling of soy sauce.

Roast Rack of Lamb, Bulghur Pilaff and Salad

The roasted lamb is a variation on ordinary lamb chops. Cooked the usual way they feel like Monday food, whereas rack of lamb, served rare, is what you might order in a restaurant.

12	small lamb chops, fixed together in sets of 3 or 4
I tsp	mustard
2 tbsp	brown sugar
½ tsp	paprika
For the bulghur pilaff:	
I cup	bulghur (cracked wheat)
I	onion
2 tbsp	oil
½ cube	chicken or beef stock
For the salad:	
I	green lettuce (like cos)
I	red tinged lettuce (radicchio or oak leaf)
4 tbsp	olive oil
I tbsp	red wine vinegar
	salt and black pepper

You will need: a roasting dish large enough to take the meat in one layer and a non-stick frying pan.
Preheat the oven to 450F, 230C, Gas 8.

Take a sharp knife and cut three diagonal lines into the fatty part of the chops. Do the same thing in the other direction, forming a diamond pattern, but not cutting deep into the meat. (This is to stop the fat curling up in the heat of the oven.) Spread the mustard over the lamb racks. Then mix the brown sugar with the paprika and sprinkle this over the mustard. Arrange the racks fairly close together, with the bone side down and the sprinkled side on top and cook for exactly 25 minutes.

Meanwhile: Take a teacup and fill it with bulghur. Chop the onion finely. Heat the oil in a large frying pan and when it is hot, throw in the onion. Stir until it starts to brown (about two or three minutes) and then add the bulghur, stirring again to mix it with the sautéed onion. Crumble the stock cube, sprinkle half of it into the cup and fill it with boiling water. Stir well and pour this into the bulghur mixture, keeping the heat high. Add another cup of boiling water, pour it over and cook until the mixture starts to bubble. Then turn off the heat and cover the pan. You can now go away and set the table. After about eight minutes the bulghur will be soft and dry and the stock should be completely absorbed. It will not spoil if you leave it a little longer.

To make the salad, wash and dry the leaves very well. (Wet lettuce and oily dressings don't mix.) Pour the dressing ingredients into a small bowl and whisk with a fork to combine the oil and vinegar. They will separate if left to stand, but can always be whisked again just before you pour the dressing over the salad at the table. If you want to make more and keep some for another time, double the quantities and pour the dressing into an empty wine bottle. Press in the cork and shake vigorously.

Now the dinner is almost ready. Make sure the plates are very hot. Take the chops out of the oven and cut down between them with a sharp knife. Spoon some of the bulghur pilaff on to each plate and arrange three chops on the side. Serve the salad separately.

Bon appétit.

The Menu

Sliced Aubergines with Garlic and Herbs

Potatoes, Crème Fraîche and Crudités

Avocado, Tomato and Mozzarella Salad

Roasted Peppers

• • •

Nectarines, Tayberries and Blackcurrants

Pears, Watercress and Blue Cheese

Mascarpone Cheese with Dates

The Techniques

Roasting vegetables

Boiling

Puréeing

The Art of Shopping

Most people do it once a week – some even boast they do it two or three times. Shopping for food is not much fun. If you go to small shops you can travel miles in seach of everything you need. One visit to a supermarket may be the answer but the weekly 'trip' is hardly the happy outing that the word implies.

The first problem is getting there. Without a car you need to have completed a weight-lifting course. With one, it should be much easier, if it weren't for the horrendous underground car parks with dank lifts. When you've left the car you can then go on to the next stage – playing slot machines with pound coins to release a trolley.

Once inside a supermarket, it's easy to get distracted. The smell of freshly baked bread coming from the in-store bakery is designed to make you spend money. All you need is a sensible loaf but you end up buying an American muffin, baked in one of those huge paper cases, with soft chocolate oozing out and spilling over the edge. "Never go shopping when you are hungry," say the diet books. But how can you choose, if you are not ?

The vast choice is part of the problem. There are over twelve thousand different items on display, so you need to be organised if the aim is to come home with enough food for a week. That means walking past the glossy green houseplants and ignoring the temptation to buy an ornamental Japanese cabbage. You have to thread yourw ay round the international fruit displays. There are boxes labelled Spain, Israel, South Africa, Morocco and Brazil – and that is just the selection of oranges.

The dairy section is a battle of wills: diet versus desire. At one end of the scale are those beastly little lumps known as slimming cottage cheese. At the other are the creams – single for coffee, double for cakes, and triple (alias clotted) for scones. Somewhere in the middle are a confusion of crème fraîche and fromage blanc, live yogurt and smatana.

Shivering past the frozen food cabinets you pick up a numbered ticket at the delicatessen. You disappear for a moment into the next aisle and spend a couple of minutes gazing at twenty new products for getting rid of stains. When you've found the one that will remove red wine, tomato sauce and grass on trousers, it's time to head back for the pâté – only to discover your number has passed.

With a full load, you reach the next stage in the obstacle race. You stagger wearily towards the checkout and join the line of trolleys. As you gaze at the pensioner's ten tins of catfood or the single vegetarian dinner nestling amid giant packs of burgers and chips, you realise you are peering into other people's lives.

Suddenly you have arrived at the moving belt. This is one of the tasks you are never trained for in school: how to unload the trolley quickly, struggle with the unopenable plastic bags and pile it all in at the other end. What is more, you are expected to look cheerful as you pay. All this calls for more co-ordination and energy than any playground game.

Fifty years ago the problems were different. In the 1940s one would queue for two hours at the greengrocer and come home with a heavy shopping bag full of root vegetables. By a stroke of luck there might be one orange. Bananas were almost unheard of. A little girl who had just arrived as a refugee from Poland was handed a banana. Her first bite was the most disappointing mouthful of her life. No-one had told her to peel it first.

In the 1960s it was hard to buy anything foreign. Vegetables that feature in television recipes today were unheard of in England thirty years ago. In a small country town, a customer with a baby in a black shiny pram asked a shopkeeper for an aubergine. He disappeared into the back of the store, saying that he wasn't sure if he had any. He came out a few minutes later, mumbling that he'd found one but it looked 'rather hard and green'. He was carrying an avocado.

Today that baby is probably a solicitor who will be looking at a very different display. He'll be wondering how to choose between a dozen different olive oils, remembering his holiday and the languid markets of Provence or Tuscany.

Shopping always seems better somewhere else. In the United States they say 'have a nice day' as they help to load bottles into bags that won't collapse. Yet their giant red apples and glossy Californian plums can never compete with an early English cox, a greengage with cracked, yellowing skin or a Victoria plum that can be stoned with one hand.

On the East Coast, in Boston, there's an incredible food store called Bread and Circus. Everything on sale is glisteningly fresh − mostly organic − and always appetising. There are twenty types of coffee bean and bunches of sweet basil; fresh cranberries and blue fish pâté. The owners have an extraordinary policy − if you buy something, take it home and find it unsatisfactory, they will give a refund with no questions asked. 'Unsatisfactory' doesn't have to mean poor quality; it can just mean that you don't like it. Imagine the Marks and Spencer policy about returning clothes, applied to food. You take home a quart of apple juice and pour out two glasses. If it's not to your taste, you simply return the rest the following day.

What a contrast this is to the computerised shopping we can expect in the future. We shall be able to scan the shelves of the local supermarket on a home television screen, punch instructions into a computer and fax the order through. In spite of the struggles, most of us would probably prefer the way it is today. Certainly, without the smell and feel of a freshly baked baguette, the stores may find it hard to sell their merchandise and will look back ruefully to the way it usedto be in the '90s.

However the food arrives in your kitchen, you may still be too tired to cook. The best plan is to put the kettle on and pick up the phone. The idea is to invite some friends to a meal tomorrow – not the sort of dinner that needs hours of preparation, more like an exercise in putting together some of the things you have bought.

This menu happens to be vegetarian and will serve four hungry people, but if you add some cooked meats or salami you can make it go further.

Sliced Aubergines with Garlic and Herbs

Nowadays everyone knows the difference between an avocado and an aubergine. These shiny purple vegetables should be firm and never wrinkled. They are often combined with cheese, tomato sauce and large quantities of oil in bubbling, gutsy dishes, but can also be served cold, like this, as a starter or salad.

I lb	450g	very glossy aubergines
		salt and pepper
3 cloves		garlic
3 tbsp		tomato purée
½ tsp		sugar
3 - 4 tbsp		olive oil
I tbsp		fresh mint
I tbsp		fresh parsley

You will need: a large shallow baking tin or a sheet of foil on an oven tray; absorbent kitchen roll; a sharp knife.

Wash and slice the aubergines into rounds about half an inch (1.5 cm) thick, spread them out on kitchen paper and sprinkle with salt. Leave them for about half an hour as this process will draw out some of the juices which may be bitter.
Preheat the oven to 375F, 190C, Gas 5.
Peel the garlic cloves and crush them. To do this you can either use a special garlic crusher or a large knife. Hold the wide end of the knife over the garlic and punch it down hard with the other hand. Chop the mint and parsley finely.
Brush the foil or baking tin with oil (or grease it with a piece of kitchen paper moistened with the oil if you have no brush). Rinse the aubergine slices and dry them very well, then arrange them in a single layer close together all over the foil or tin. Mix the crushed garlic with the tomato purée, sugar, salt and pepper and spoon a little of this mixture on to each slice. Brush over the rest of the olive oil and sprinkle with the chopped herbs. Bake for about 30 minutes or until the aubergine slices are soft. Carefully lift them off (with a palette knife if you have one) and leave to cool. Serve the slices as a starter with crisp warm French bread or as a salad with cold meat.

Potatoes, Crème Fraîche and Crudités

French crème fraîche is thick and spoonable and goes well with the crunchy raw vegetables.

I lb	450g	new potatoes or 4 large old potatoes
4		carrots
½ lb	225g	sugar peas
4 small		cooked beetroot
8 tbsp		crème fraîche

You will need: a medium sized saucepan and a strainer or colander.

Scrub the potatoes and cut large ones into thick slices. (Potatoes can be boiled in cold or hot water – some people even insist on using bottled water, but the taste depends more on the variety of potato than the water.) Anyway, make sure they are covered, add a little salt and boil till they are tender (about 15 minutes). You can tell when they are done by poking them with a sharp knife. Drain them throughthe colander and spr inkle with some black pepper.

While they are cooking you can prepare the other vegetables. Peel or scrape the carrots and cut them into sticks. Peel the beetroot and cut into chunks. Just wash the sugar peas and pinch off the ends.

Spoon the crème fraîche into the middle of a large plate and arrange the potatoes (warm or cold) and the vegetables in piles around the outside. If you feel artistic you can swirl a piece of beetroot across the crème fraîche which makes a pretty pink marbled effect. (Even if you knew how to boil potatoes before, you probably didn't know that beetroot is an instant dye).

Avocado, Tomato and Mozzarella Salad

This is another name for a famous salad called Insalata Tricolore, named after the red, green and white of the Italian national flag. The best mozzarella is made from buffalo milk. Cut avocados turn black if they are left exposed to the air for more than about half an hour. You can avoid this by squeezing lemon juice over them but it is better to have everything else ready and assemble it all at the last minute.

8 oz	225g	firm sweet tomatoes or cherry tomatoes
I pot		mozzarella balls or a bag of buffalo mozzarella
2		ripe avocados
5 or 6 leaves		fresh basil
3 tbsp		extra virgin olive oil (the best)
I		lemon (optional)

Slice the tomatoes and the mozzarella, or if you are using the balls and cherry tomatoes leave them both whole. Cut the avocados in half and carefully take out the stones with the point of a sharp knife. Peel off the skins and cut the avocado flesh into long thin pieces. Arrange the avocado, tomato and mozzarella on a large shallow plate. Tear the basil leaves into pieces and sprinkle them on top. (Do this just before serving. Doing it too soon or cutting them with a blunt knife discolours them and spoils their texture.) Drizzle over the olive oil and serve immediately.

Roasted Peppers

Supermarkets often sell peppers in packs of yellow, green and red. The green ones have a bitter flavour (because they aren't ripe) while the others are sweet, so although the combination looks pretty, it's best to choose the summer colours. Then there is the question of peeling them — the skins will come off, with difficulty, after they are cooked, but like tomatoes I don't think the skin is unpleasant, unless it becomes detached.

3 or 4	yellow, red or orange peppers
3 - 4 tbsp	olive oil
	salt and pepper

You will need: a large shallow baking tin.
Preheat the oven to 375F, 190C, Gas 5.

Wash and dry the peppers and cut them in half, removing all the loose seeds, the green stems and the pale membranes which form lines along the inside. Then cut them into strips – as wide or narrow as you like. Sprinkle the oil over the tin and arrange the peppers in a single layer, turning them over to make sure they are coated with a little oil. Cook for 30 to 40 minutes when the tips will be brown at the edges. Spoon the peppers, with any orangey oil, into a bowl, season well and leave to cool. They can be covered and left in the fridge overnight but the flavour is better if they are not too cold.

Nectarines, Tayberries and Blackcurrants

The lightly cooked blackcurrants are passed through a sieve to make a sauce. If you can't find the other fruit, you can use peaches or strawberries; just choose whatever looks freshest.

8 oz	225g	blackcurrants
I tbsp		sugar (or more if you like things sweet)
4 large		ripe nectarines
I lb	450g	tayberries, raspberries, or blueberries

You will need: a small saucepan; a sieve and a large bowl.

First prepare the blackcurrants. Cut off the spindly stems and ends, wash the currants and put them in a small pan with the sugar and two tablespoons of water. Heat until the water boils and the juices from the currants start to run. Leave them to cool.

Put the nectarines in a large bowl and pour over enough boiling water to cover them. Almost immediately lift them out carefully and take off the skins with a sharp knife. Slice the nectarines, discarding the stones, and arrange them in a glass bowl. Spray a little water over the tayberries but don't let them get soggy. Drain them on a paper towel and then spoon the berries over the nectarine slices. Press the blackcurrants through a fine sieve and pour this purée over the fruit. Cover the bowl and keep it in the fridge.

Pears with Watercress and Blue Cheese

This dish can be served at any time, as a starter at the beginning of a meal or a savoury at the end. Sandwiched between slices of fresh granary bread, it makes a great lunch.

I bunch		very fresh watercress
6 oz	175g	pipo crem, blue brie or dolcelatte cheese
3		ripe comice or William pears

Wash the watercress and remove the stalks. Cut the cheese into thick slices. Peel, core and slice the pears. Arrange everything on a large, flat dish. (A squeeze of lemon juice will stop the pears discolouring.)

Mascarpone Cheese with Dates

This recipe is not exactly a dessert, but a treat. This soft, sweet cream cheese from Italy used to come in small pots but now seems to come only in the 250g size. If you get bored filling the dates, the rest of the cheese is great in sandwiches with slices of crunchy carrot and some crushed fresh green peppercorns.

I box	dried dates
I pot	mascarpone cheese

Cut the dates lengthwise across the top. Take care not to split them in half, but bend them open and lift out the stones. With a small teaspoon, spoon a little mascarpone cheese into each one and ar range the dates on a plate.

The Menu

Chilli Puffs

Lemony Bean Salad

Bean Soup

• • •

Brisket of Beef with Chestnuts

• • •

Apple or Peach Pie

Crêpes with Grand Marnier

The Techniques

Basic pastry

Cooking pulses

Slow-braising meat

Making pancakes

Frozen Wastes

"When my mother had to get dinner for eight, she'd just make enough for sixteen and serve half." This was a novel approach to catering from Gracie Allen, one of the early television comediennes. Making meals was a full time job in the days of resident cooks. Margaret Powell described her routine as a cook housekeeper in a book called "Below Stairs". She wrote without complaint: "Preparing food was the sole purpose of our lives."

In the early days of home freezers, the whole point of owning one was to simplify the task of feeding the family. Large white chests began to appear in suburban garages across the land. The owners would then buy half a cow and embark on 'chain cooking'. Twenty pounds of mince had to be turned into burgers, bolognaise and lasagne and mothers would rush exhausted to the school gates at four o'clock having spent the day cooking enough food for a month. They were not cooking for an imagined famine. The purpose of the intensive freezer filling exercise was to save time and money. But it occasionally went wrong. As well as sides of beef there were massive, catering-size blocks of cheddar cheese. No-one revealed that the trick was to cut them up before freezing. It needed hammer, chisel and saw to reduce a solid block to usable pieces.

Since the arrival of cook-chill products, frozen food has lost much of its appeal. Late-opening shops have also reduced the need to keep stocks at home. If you like cooking it is still a good idea to make double quantities – one for today, one for next week, but it needs some thought if you are trying to produce a delicious meal for unexpected guests at an hour's notice.

Most of us use the freezer like an attic – a good place to keep things that may never be needed. Slimming experts often suggest freezing leftovers to avoid temptation but fail to recognise the flaws in this advice. A determined but miserable dieter can easily find ways of demolishing a solid block of chocolate sauce, and home-made buttery biscuits are perfect eaten standing up, shivering by the open freezer door.

Most leftovers are never as useful as you hope. Suppose you make a summer pudding in July - there's no point eating it in August when you can still buy all the fresh berries, so you leave it until December by which time it is far less appetising and has probably deteriorated. To make Danish pastries involves a lengthy process with a buttered yeast dough. A wonderful smell of cinnamon sugar and warm fruit eventually fills the kitchen after hours of rolling, folding and chilling.

The baked crescents and squares can then be packed away and stored. For when? They're too good to offer the plumber when he is fixing the washing machine and most children would prefer chocolate digestive biscuits.

The great ice-box has come a long way since the days of conserving ice cream. It keeps some food in perfect limbo and gives people a squirrel-like satisfaction. But it can also be a pain. A friend once spent a miserable weekend alone while her husband was salmon fishing in Scotland. He passed the days happily dreaming by the lochs waiting for a catch, while her job was to meet the trains and freeze the fish that he dispatched.

All but the most modern freezers need to be defrosted occasionally. This involves bowls of hot water and towels all over the floor. I once lost a treasured opal ring. Months later, it turned up in a pool of defrosting ice. On a dark night, it must have dropped down between the packs of lamb chops. The ring was quite unharmed, so the freezer might be a safe place to keep the family jewels.

What else should you store? The answer is whatever helps to make a meal. The menu for this chapter contains some new skills, but if you're short of time, or not ready to try something harder, then the recipes can be made using the bought equivalent. The easiest time to experiment is when you are not cooking for tonight's dinner, so all these dishes can be prepared ahead and stored for another time.

Before the recipes, here are some small things which take up little space and are worth storing:

- **Simple ice cubes**

  Swirl a couple of cubes into a fatty gravy. After a minute you can lift out the ice and the fat which will have hardened around it, leaving a much-improved gravy underneath.

- **Ginger**

  Keep a piece of peeled ginger root in labelled wrap and grate it, frozen, into sauces and curries. It grates more easily when hard and the flavour is just as strong.

- **Herbs**

  You can buy frozen, chopped herbs in small, re-closeable boxes. If you keep them for too long the smell permeates everything in the freezer. More useful is a bunch of fresh, washed parsley which can be frozen and crunched up with one hand to sprinkle into a stuffing.

- **Cream**

  Better than keeping pots of cream in the fridge are packs of frozen cream sticks. A single stick of whipping cream can be swirled, frozen, straight into a soup or sauce. A whole pack of double cream can be defrosted and whipped up for a cake filling.

- **Wine**

  The morning after a dinner party is not the moment to finish off the last inch in the bottle. Pour it into a small pot and freeze it. Since it doesn't turn into solid rock you can chip off a few flakes to improve a sauce.

- **Small fruits**

  Raspberries and strawberries are too watery to freeze whole. Spread red or black currants on a large tray. Once hard, the stalks will fall off and the currants can be stored in a bag. Even easier are blueberries which have no stalks.

- **Spinach**

  Frozen, chopped spinach is watery and tasteless. Leaf spinach is all right, mixed with cheddar or ricotta cheese. Best of all is fresh, but the large leaves need as much washing as a pair of sandy swimming trunks. Whichever you use it disappears into a small heap when cooked.

Pastry

If the weather or your hands are warm, it's better to chill the dough for half an hour. You can freeze it if you want to, but a solid block takes too long to defrost, so it's best to roll it out and use it in a pie or flan case.

8 oz	225g	plain flour
5 oz	140g	butter or hard margarine
I		egg yolk
4 tbsp		cold water

You will need: a rolling pin and a palette knife. (Using the wrong tools, like a milk bottle and an ordinary knife, will give you the equivalent of a rough patch of grass instead of a lawn.)

Most pastry recipes give instructions to add "enough water to make the dough easy to roll". This often results in a sticky mess that needs extra flour, or a dough that is so tough that it cracks. When cooking chips, or boiled potatoes, the exact amount of liquid is not crucial. With pastry, it's far better to be exact.

Cut the butter into very small pieces and rub it into the flour with your fingers until the mixture is crumbly. There shouldn't be any large lumps, nor should it be sticky. Mix the egg yolk with the water and quickly stir it into the flour mixture. With your hands, form the dough into a ball. If it seems very soft, cover it and put it in the fridge for at least half an hour. If not sprinkle a little flour on to a cold surface and place the dough in the middle.

Cut the pastry into two halves and roll it out. If the rolling pin sticks, don't sprinkle more flour on to the dough, but dust the pin with flour instead. The pastry should end up about the thickness of a pound coin. Carefully slide the palette knife round the edges and then right under the pastry until it comes away from the work surface. Now it is ready to use.

Chilli Puffs

These can be made in advance. The rounds of pastry are filled with spicy minced meat and then chilled or frozen. The final cooking can be done straight from the freezer. The recipe makes about 15 – 20 puffs.

8 oz	225g	lean beef or lamb, minced
I tbsp		oil
I		onion
½ pt	300ml	beef stock (or ½ stock cube dissolved in water)
¼ tsp		chilli powder
I tbsp		tomato purée
I quantity		pastry (page 36)
I		egg

You will need: a non-stick frying pan; a rolling pin; a palette knife; a baking sheet and a round 3" (7.5 cm) cutter.

First make the meat filling. Chop the onion finely. Fry the minced beef or lamb in the pan over medium heat, turning it frequently until it loses its red colour. Add the chopped onion, with a little oil if the pan is dry, turning up the heat until the meat and onion are brown.

Sprinkle the beef with the chilli powder and pour on the stock and the tomato purée. Stir well, and when it bubbles turn down the heat and simmer for about half an hour. When the meat is cooked, the stock will almost have evaporated. Spoon the meat filling onto a large plate and leave to get quite cold.

Roll out the pastry, slide the palette knife underneath to loosen it, and then make rounds using the cutter. Put a spoonful of the meat filling into each puff and press the edges together to form a crescent. Make a couple of small slits in each one with the tip of a sharp knife. (This is to let the air escape while the puffs cook.) If you want to freeze them, arrange them on a tray, and when they are solid, store them in a plastic bag.

To cook the puffs:
Preheat the oven to 425F, 220C, Gas 7.

Break the egg into a glass and whisk it lightly with a fork. Arrange the chilled or frozen puffs on an ungreased baking sheet. Brush with a little beaten egg and cook for 20 – 30 minutes or until they are golden brown and crisp. Serve them hot or warm, but never reheat them in the microwave as they go limp.

Lemony Bean Salad

The hard beans have a smooth shininess which changes magically once they are cooked. You can make this salad by simply opening a can but dealing with the raw ones will give you a much larger quantity and requires only a little patience. It is worth cooking the whole packet because it is no more trouble than making half.

I lb	450g	dried haricot beans
I		lemon
3 tbsp		olive oil
½ tsp		dijon mustard
I		garlic clove
		salt and pepper

You will need: a large saucepan; a strainer or a colander; a bowl and a lemon zester or grater.

Soaking and cooking the beans: Dried beans have to be soaked and then boiled vigorously for ten minutes, to remove possible toxins. (I don't know anyone who has died of bean poisoning, but it's better to be safe.) You can either soak the haricot beans in cold water overnight, or cover them with boiling water and leave for about an hour. This softens them before you start the cooking process. Choose a large pan as the soaking makes them swell. When they have doubled in size pour off the soaking liquid and cover with fresh water but no salt, since this tends to toughen the beans. Bring the water to the boil and cook for ten minutes, then turn down the heat and simmer for about 45 minutes or until they are tender. Drain all the beans through the strainer into the bowl, keeping the liquid. Use half the beans for the salad and reserve the rest for another time.

To freeze: put the cooled beans into a plastic bag and the liquid into a covered pot.

To make the salad, first prepare a lemony dressing. Remove the zest of the lemon with a gadget that makes fine strips, or grate the skin. Mix together the oil, crushed garlic and seasonings and whisk in the juice of half the lemon. While the beans are still warm pour over the dressing and leave to cool. Decorate with the lemon zest or grated lemon and serve as a starter or with green salads as a side dish.

Bean Soup

For this velvety purée you can either use some cooked haricot beans from the previous recipe or use butter beans. These are larger and flatter, have a slightly different taste but work in exactly the same way.

8 oz	225g	cooked butter beans
2 -3 tbsp		oil
8 oz	225g	carrots (2 or 3)
10 oz	275g	onions (2 large)
2 sticks		celery
I pt	570 ml	beef or chicken stock
		salt, pepper
½ tsp		paprika
few leaves		fresh coriander

You will need: a large saucepan and a liquidizer, food processor or a large sieve.

Soak and cook the butter beans according to the instructions on the packet, or as for the haricot beans. Peel the carrots and the onions and wash the celery well. Chop all the vegetables into fairly small pieces.

Put the oil in the bottom of the pan, heat until it sizzles when you throw in a small piece of carrot and then toss in the vegetable pieces. Turn them around and fry for a few minutes over high heat. Then add the cooked beans with the liquid and the stock and continue cooking until the liquid starts to bubble. After about ten minutes when the vegetables are tender blend the soup in a liquidizer or food processor, or even better press it through a sieve. The idea is to get a velvety smooth purée. The processors are fine but the sieve separates the skins from the beans leaving a finer purée. Add a little more soup stock or water to make about two pints altogether and check the seasoning. Pour the hot soup into bowls and sprinkle each one with some paprika and a few coriander leaves.

(To make the soup using frozen beans, add the beans with their liquid to the sautéed vegetables and cook over very low heat until the vegetables and beans are soft. Then purée as above.)

Brisket of Beef with Chestnuts

Lurking in the freezer cabinets of a few selected supermarkets are bags of frozen chestnuts. Fresh ones need to be roasted and peeled and although the brown outer skin comes off quite easily, the thin inner layer leaves you with burnt fingers and broken nails.

2-3 tbsp		oil
3 lbs	1.5 kg	rolled brisket or beef top rib
2		onions, peeled and cut into quarters
¾ pt	425 ml	boiling water
1		beef stock cube
8 oz	225g	frozen chestnuts
		salt, pepper

You will need: a non stick frying pan and a large lidded casserole.

Put the oil in the frying pan and brown the beef over medium heat for a few minutes, turning it over to make sure all the sides are seared. This initial cooking helps to keep the juices in. While it is cooking, throw in the quartered onions to fill up the spaces in the pan, otherwise the oil tends to burn. Turn the onions until they are beginning to brown too. Transfer the meat and the onions to a deep casserole dish and season them with salt and pepper. Crumble the stock cube into the boiling water and pour a few tablespoons into the frying pan, stirring it around. This is called 'deglazing' and just means incorporating any meaty bits into the gravy.

Pour this deglazed liquid and the rest of the stock over the meat, cover the casserole and cook at 350F, 180 C, Gas 4 for about two hours. If the casserole has a well fitting lid the gravy shouldn't evaporate too much, but check anyway after about an hour. Turn the joint of meat over if the top seems dry and add a little more water.

Add the frozen chestnuts, pushing them down so they are covered by the stock and leave the casserole to cook for a further half hour. When the beef is cooked the liquid will be slightly reduced and thickened by the chestnuts. Brisket of beef is sometimes fatty so you might prefer to remove the fat which will form a translucent layer over the gravy. Alternatively cool the whole casserole completely and chill in the fridge overnight. The fat will then harden and can be lifted off the following day. To reheat it, cook the beef over low heat until the gravy is bubbling and the meat is hot.

Apple or Peach Pie

Of course you can buy a ready-cooked pie and reheat it. But if you make your own (even with bought pastry) it will smell and taste quite different.

I lb	450g	bought or home–made pastry
1¼ lbs	575g	cooking apples or firm peaches
2 - 4 tbsp		sugar
¼ tsp		cinnamon
I		egg white

You will need: a rolling pin; a palette knife; an 8 inch (21cm) flan tin, preferably with a removable base, and a pastry brush.
Preheat the oven to 425F, 220C, Gas 7.

Peel and core the apples and cut them into slices. If you are using peaches, cover them with boiling water for half a minute and the skinsshould slip off easily . Slice the flesh and remove the stones.

Roll out the pastry, sliding the palette knife underneath to ease it off the work surface. Lift half of it into the flan tin pressing the pastry well into the base, overlapping the sides. Be careful not to stretch it. Using the rolling pin, roll across the top, pressing down lightly to cut off the edge.

Fill the pastry-lined tin with the sliced fruit. Sprinkle over a few tablespoons of sugar and the cinnamon. (The apples will need to be sweetened more than peaches.) Lift the remaining pastry over the fruit and press it down at the edges using the rolling pin to seal it. Anyspar e bits will fall off. Whisk the egg white lightly with a fork until it looks frothy and brush a little over the top of the pie. Sprinkle over another spoonful of sugar and cut a few slits in the top of the pastry for the steam to escape. You can make an apple design if you like drawing. Bake for about 40 minutes.

Leave the pie to cool slightly before removing it from the tin. To do this, ease round the edges with a knife and gently press up the base.

Pancakes

Making pancakes (or crêpes, in French) is not quick. It isn't the filling or the showy part with the flambé pan that takes the time; it is making the things in the first place. Forget about tossing them, because half of them will end up on the floor. Once you've mastered the knack of thin pancakes, you can double the recipe and make enough for two meals in the time it takes to listen to a Mozart piano concerto.

4 oz	125g	plain flour
1		egg
¼ pt	150 ml	milk
¼ pt	150 ml	iced water
3 fl oz	75ml	oil

You will need: an electric mixer or liquidizer (optional); a small heat resistant jug; a small frying pan; a palette knife and some sheets of greaseproof paper.

Sieve the flour into a bowl. Break in the egg and whisk in a little of the milk with an electric mixer or a hand whisk. Continue adding the rest of the liquid with a teaspoon of the oil, and beat until the batter is smooth. (Alternatively you can use a liquidizer to make sure there are no lumps.) If you have time, leave it in the fridge for about half an hour.

Cover the base of the pan with a few tablespoons of oil and turn on the heat. Almost immediately poursome oil back into the jug, leaving a thin film covering the pan. Stir the pancake batter and spoon in enough to cover the base of the pan – not enough and there will be wispy trails round the edges – too much and there will be a thick pool in the centre. The batter should sizzle as it touches the oil and very quickly it will start to cook and will change from almost white to pale yellow. There may be some bubbles on the surface.

Now it will begin to look like a pancake. With a palette knife carefully ease round the outside, sliding the knife underneath to stop it sticking. Turn it over and cook the other side for a few minutes, or until it begins to brown. (You can tell by lifting up a corner and looking underneath.) The first pancake will probably not be brilliant. Oil the pan again, as before, and make another one which will be better. Carry on with the rest of the batter, pouring some oil in and out each time and arranging the cooked pancakes on the paper. (Don't pile them on top of each other or they will stick.)

To freeze: when they are cold, stack the pancakes in between sheets of greaseproof paper. Store them in clingfilm or a plastic bag.

Crêpes with Grand Marnier

This is not the traditional 'crêpes suzette' recipe where pancakes are heated and flamed in a syrupy sauce. These are not too sweet and go well with strawberries in summer. In winter you can serve them with sliced oranges and bring out the flavour by using fresh orange juice instead of milk in the pancake recipe. The crêpes can, of course, be made in advance but make sure the guests are ready and the plates are hot before you start to heat the liqueur.

2 - 4 tbsp	oil (unscented, i.e. not olive or nut)
8	crêpes
6 tbsp	Grand Marnier
1 - 2 tbsp	sugar

You will need: a large frying pan; a metal soup ladle and a box of matches.

Heat a tablespoon of oil in the pan and when it is hot, slide in two of the pancakes. Sprinkle with a little of the sugar. Immediately fold the pancakes in half, then in half again.Slide them o ver to one side and continue heating the remaining pancakes in the same way. Keep them warm over very low heat while you do the next step. Pour the Grand Marnier into the soup ladle and heat it carefully over a flame or high heat. When it bubbles, light it with a match (standing as far back as possible) and pour the flaming liqueur quickly over the crêpes.

(If you are using frozen pancakes, separate the papers and lay them out to defrost quickly. When you can bend one easily without cracking it, it is ready to use.)

The Menu

'Grilled' Peppers in Oil

Broccoli with Hazelnut Vinaigrette

Asparagus

• • •

Salmon Steaks with Mushrooms

• • •

Stewed Rhubarb or Gooseberries

Orange Sabayon Sauce

The Techniques

Cooking in the microwave:

Steaming vegetables; poaching fish

Stewing fruit; making sauces

The Misunderstood Microwave

The manufacturers of complicated machines have finally given in. They realise that the technology is too complicated for average mortals to understand. To set the video you just need to punch in a set of numbers without even looking at the clock. The thinking process has been totally removed. It is the same with microwave ovens. You only need to lift a frozen dinner into the machine and it will calculate the weight and cooking time and switch off when the job is done.

Half the cooks in Britain own a machine that is hardly used because they believe it needs a knowledge of computers instead of cooking. The microwave oven stands proudly in the kitchen, bleeping away to announce that a dish is done, leaving most people totally unaware of its immense potential. In fact, it is much harder to master auto weight combinations and heat sensors than to cook something simple from scratch.

There are two basic features which make a microwave oven different from a conventional one: it cooks with moist heat and speed. It is brilliant for steaming vegetables and poaching fish. It is the only sensible way to make a sponge pudding and the fastest method of cooking fruit.

Manufacturers somehow managed to get the message of speed across by promoting the four-minute jacket potato but they forgot to say that it was no more like a real baked potato than a piece of stale bread is like crisp toast.

In the early days the news spread fast that the magic machines could defrost chickens and heat milk. Publishers commissioned food writers to compile microwave cookbooks and this is where the trouble started. There were recipes for roast beef and fruit bread. Much effort was put into disguising the pallid results and concealing the leaden loaves with colouring and frosting. Each step had to be done in the microwave – no more fried onions or sautéed mushrooms. Every dish in every meal had to be produced quicker using the new method. It hardly seemed to matter that scrambled eggs were rubbery and meat was tough.

So why try to cook with a microwave? Cooking involves tasting, stirring, watching and developing techniques to make different foods respond to heat. A microwave is an invaluable tool for certain stages in this process. It is often better than other methods or sometimes just as good, but it involves far less work.

One of the reasons microwaves have a bad name is that they are used undiscerningly in fast food restaurants. Reheating a sausage roll just makes the pastry go soggy. At the other end of the catering business, the machines are totally banned from the kitchens of top hotels. The chefs in good restaurants have no need to deal with small quantities or to consider the question of saving time and effort. It doesn't matter to them if a fish takes three minutes or thirty to cook - the customers will have a drink while they are waiting. Nor do they care that fruit can be cooked and served in the same dish, without watching it or worrying that it might burn. In a good establishment there is no shortage of sous-chefs and washers-up. Cooking at home is different. There are few people who relish the chores of tending simmering pans and washing them up afterwards.

When you buy your first car it certainly changes your life. But it doesn't mean that you'll never go for a walk again. In the same way, when you buy a microwave oven, you shouldn't expect it to do all the tasks of a conventional oven and hob. It's an extra kitchen tool. But you have to use it sensibly. It's like the recipe for cooking a salmon in the dishwasher. It is certainly possible, if you wrap the fish in three layers of foil, then plastic, to 'cook' it on a cool wash for about an hour and a half. But there are better ways to do it.

To see how the machine works, start with a slab of butter, a bar of chocolate and a Bramley cooking apple. This is not a recipe – it's a series of experiments. The word 'high' refers to full power.

- Take about 1 oz (25g) butter from the fridge and two saucers. Put half of it on one and cook on **high** for 10 seconds. It should now be soft enough to spread. Do the same with the the other half and cook for 40 seconds. You should now have a melted pool. This shows that small amounts take a very short time to come to room temperature and not much longer to make them useful in cooking. Don't worry that it also shows what a difference 30 seconds can make. With practice you will be able to judge for yourself.

- Now break off about 2 oz (50g) good plain chocolate and put it on a small plate. Microwave it on **high** for about a minute. Take it out carefully because the plate may be hot and stir the chocolate until it is completely melted. The traditional way of melting chocolate is to heat it in a bowl over a pan of simmering water. This is quicker and cleaner and there is no risk of water splattering into the bowl which can ruin the chocolate.

• Next peel and core the apple and cut it into thin slices. Arrange these
in a shallow dish and cook on **high** for 2 minutes. The slices should
be just soft but should not have disintegrated. Sprinkle them with
some sugar, put a cover on the dish or use microwaveable cling film
and continue cooking on **high** for another 2 minutes. Carefully lift
off the lid or film (because of the steam underneath) and you will
see stewed apple. You just need to stir and mash it slightly with a fork
to make apple sauce.

These three examples show how to use the new technique in
baking. In many ways the microwave is the greatest advance in food
preparation since the introduction of gas in the 1900s. The French
have realised this for some time. Over three years ago "Elle" magazine
published articles about the 'cordon bleu in your kitchen' referring
to the excellent results with fish and vegetables. The Americans
produced the first microwave encyclopaedia but forgot to edit out the
more crazy notions. If you heat fat for five minutes, the spattering
takes another ten minutes to wash off. The idea of stirring sauces
through a slit in clingfilm is nonsensical. Worst of all is attempting to
deep fry in a microwave. The recipe for tempura needs strong nerves
and a handy first-aid kit.

To find out why the new method is so good for poaching a salmon
or steaming asparagus, you need to do an experiment with liquid.
The more you put in a microwave oven, the longer it takes to cook.
(This applies to everything, but especially water.) Half a glass of water
will boil in about a minute while a pint, (cooked in a milk bottle just
for fun) will take about five. If you cover vegetables or fish with lots
of water they will take longer than if you sprinkle over a few
spoonfuls. Incidentally, it is better to add salt to the water, rather than
sprinkle it directly on to the food, where it dries.

To cook some broccoli on the hob, you would boil it in a large pot
of simmering water, drain it and then throw all the liquid away. The
old way to cook asparagus involved tying the stems with string and
standing the asparagus upright in a steamer, being careful not to
damage the tips. Half an hour later, with a room full of steam, you
would burn your fingers lifting the bunch on to a warm plate.

Cooking vegetables in a microwave is the first step in learning to
master its capabilities. By the end of the book you should be using it
without hesitation to make many things simpler.

Before you begin, you need to understand about the equipment
you will need. You can do without large cumbersome items like a
vegetable steamer, fish kettle or bain-marie. Instead, you can cook in
almost anything - paper, china, plastic or glass (as long as it's not foil

or metal, since both of these cause sparks in the machine). Since most foods cook better if they are covered, it's a good idea to buy either a shallow plastic container with a vented lid, or simply use your own plates and dishes and buy a large round cover that will fit over the top.

The crucial question of 'how long does it take?' can be answered once you have started practising and learning how your particular machine responds to the foods you put in it. The recipes here have all been tested on a microwave with a turntable and a high power output (750W). If yours is lower, you may need to cook foods for slightly longer. Precooked food always carries warnings about making sure it is cooked thoroughly. With fresh food, like fish or vegetables, there is no danger if the result is undercooked. It's more a matter of taste than health.

Any microwave book or manual will tell you about power output, wattages and standing times. It's like playing a new game – the page with the rules seems so long and boring, you just want to get started moving the pieces round the board. So this is what you do. Start by cooking everything on full power or **high** and remember one thing: you can always stop the cooking by opening the door and carry on again till the food is done. It's better than trying to save something which is overcooked. So the first message is "Watch and see".

For all these recipes you will need: a shallow dish, either plastic, glass or china with no metal or gold trim, with a vented lid (i.e. with a hole). Alternatively, but not so good, use microwaveable clingfilm with a couple of slits to release the steam.

'Grilled' Peppers in Oil

Instructions for grilling peppers usually involve charring them under intense heat until they go black. The microwave method keeps the bright colours and gives an excellent and surprisingly 'grilled' flavour. They are good warm or cool, but should only be seasoned after cooking.

I lb	450g	red, orange or yellow peppers (about 3)
3 tbsp		olive oil
		salt, black pepper

Wash and dry the peppers. Remove the stems and the white membrane and seeds which are inside. Either leave them in halves or cut them into strips. Toss them in the olive oil and cook, uncovered, on **high** for about 3 minutes. If you like them softer, and want to remove the skins, continue cooking for a minute or so. Sprinkle with salt and black pepper and pour over the juice before serving.

Broccoli with Hazelnut Vinaigrette

The broccoli can be served hot or cold. In both cases, sprinkle over the vinaigrette and some black pepper at the last minute.

I lb	450g	broccoli
		salt, black pepper
For the vinaigrette:		
4 tbsp		hazelnut oil
2 tbsp		sunflower oil
2 tbsp		white wine vinegar
¼ tsp		mustard
		pinch sugar

Trim the ends of the broccoli and cut them into florets leaving the stems long. They will cook better if you cut them into even sizes. Wash and arrange the pieces in a shallow dish. Sprinkle 3 tablespoons of lightly salted water over the broccoli. Cover and cook on **high** for 4 minutes. Uncover it as soon as it is cooked, otherwise the colour fades. (If you are serving the broccoli cold, refresh it briefly with cold water, and drain.)

To make the vinaigrette, put all the ingredients into an empty wine bottle with a cork (if you don't have one, a screw top jar will do). Shake the sauce vigorously until it is thick.

Asparagus

A cool dip, like mayonnaise or crème fraîche, is good if you are serving the asparagus cold. To eat it hot, you need large napkins.

I lb	450g	fresh asparagus
4 tbsp		water
		salt, pepper
2 - 3 oz	50 – 75g	butter
3 tbsp		chopped fresh herbs (chervil, parsley or dill)

Trim off the tough ends of the asparagus and scrape the last few inches of the stems with a vegetable peeler. Wash them briefly and then drain. This preparation can be done in advance. The actual cooking should be done at the last minute. Arrange the asparagus in a single layer in an oval or rectangular dish. Sprinkle over the lightly salted water, cover and cook on **high** for about 6 minutes. While it is cooking, mash the herbs into the butter with a fork. The asparagus tips should be tender and the stems should no longer be tough when poked with a sharp knife.

If you are serving the asparagus hot, drain off the water, arrange the vegetables on hot plates and dot pieces of the herb butter over the tips. It will melt immediately, so make sure everyone is sitting down. This amount serves two as a starter. If you want to cook more, repeat the process and just keep the first lot warm while you do so.

Salmon Steaks with Mushrooms

This dish serves two people. Cooking four steaks will take longer, but not twice as long.

2 medium sized		steaks of salmon
3 tbsp		white wine
		salt, pepper
6 oz	175g	mushrooms (oyster, chestnut etc)
1 oz	25g	butter

Wash the mushrooms and dry them with a paper towel. Place the fish in a shallow dish. (The way you arrange it is quite important because the centre always cooks slower in a microwave, so lay them side by side with the narrow end of one next to the broad end of the other.) Season with a little salt and pepper and pour over the wine. Cover and cook for 2 – 3 minutes on **high**. (To cook four salmon steaks, increase the cooking time to 4 minutes on **high**.)

Meanwhile, melt the butter in a small frying pan, cut the mushrooms into thick slices and sauté them over high heat until they are brown. Test to see if the salmon is cooked by pressing the tip of a knife near the bone. If it looks underdone, cook for another minute. The time depends on the thickness of the fish, but take care not to overcook it, or it will be dry. Lift the steaks out of the cooking liquid on to warmed plates and surround with the mushrooms.

Stewed Rhubarb or Gooseberries

The method is the same for all fruits. Timing depends on how many you are cooking, how soft they were to start with and as always, on the power output of your oven. Remember as usual, to start off with a few minutes, see if they are soft and if not, continue for another minute or so. It never matters if you open the door and look to see what is happening.

1 lb	450g	rhubarb or gooseberries
2 tbsp		sugar (or more, depending on taste)

For rhubarb, wash it, and cut off any tatty looking bits at the ends. Holding several sticks at a time on a board, slice them into even sized pieces about an inch (2.5 cm) long. Put the rhubarb pieces on the bottom of a shallow dish, sprinkle with about 3 tablespoons of sugar and cover with a vented lid or a piece of microwaveable film. Cook on **high** for about four minutes, but move the pieces around after two to make sure they cook evenly. The longer you cook it the softer and more mushy it gets. You may want to add more sugar, so taste the clear red juice before it cools.

For gooseberries, cut off the bits at the top and bottom (called top and tailing, officially) and wash the fruit. Arrange them in a single layer in a shallow dish, sprinkle with sugar and cook for 2 – 3 minutes, covered, until they soften. If you cook the berries too much they will collapse; even this isn't a disaster. Press them through a sieve and you will have gooseberry purée – a brilliant tart sauce which goes well with fish.

Orange Sabayon Sauce

Cooking eggs in a microwave needs care. Adding a little flour to an egg-based custard, like this, helps to stabilise it, but to stop it curdling you must stir it frequently. Opening the door to do this is more inconvenient than cooking over direct heat. However, the custard cooks quickly and whereas it would stick to a saucepan, it will never stick to the bowl.

2		egg yolks
2 tbsp		sugar
¼ pt	150ml	orange juice (from about 3 oranges)
I tsp		flour
2 tbsp		Grand Marnier or Cointreau

You will need: a medium size bowl and a strainer.

In the bowl mix the egg yolks with the sugar and the flour, making a thick paste. Squeeze the oranges and strain the juice into the egg mixture, stirring it well. Microwave the sauce on **medium** power for about 3 minutes, stirring it 3 or 4 times until it thickens. When it coats the back of the spoon and is thick, it is done. Stand the bowl in cold water to cool it and then stir in the orange liqueur.

The Menus

Chunky Beef and Vegetable Soup

• • •

Golden Gravy Chicken

Slow-Roasted Duck

• • •

Winter Fruit Platter with Ricciarelli

Courgette and Almond Soup

• • •

Pasta with Asparagus and Nuts

Barbecued Fresh Tuna

• • •

Apple Cheesecakes and Blackberry Sauce

The Techniques

Meat and vegetable stocks for soup

Braising and roasting poultry

Cooking pasta and grilling or barbecuing fish

Oven and microwave baking

A Good Reputation

My father hated going out. He had a mischievous streak and would say embarrassing things at dinner parties. My mother liked company and came to terms with the problem by entertaining her friends at home.

She is a marvellous pastry cook and used to turn out eclairs and brioches, nougat baskets and marron tartlets as regular fare for tea time. We lived in a house in Walm Lane, Cricklewood, which had a huge unheated living-room in the front and a small sitting room with a coal fire in the back.

I would come home to the unmistakeable smell of what was called coffee cake. As the buttery dough baked, it doubled in size and turnedinto a s weet loaf, halfway between bread and cake. It had an indefinable taste – a hint of cinnamon or vanilla – and was thickly spread with more butter. It was called coffee cake but we always had it with tea. To this day I have never been able to recapture the exact taste that would remind me of when I was seventeen, sitting by that fire.

My mother had a reputation for serving the best meals in North West London. Apart from the cakes she made beef casseroles and stuffed joints of lamb. There was always a huge stock pot full of bones simmering on the stove – either chunky beef bones or the carcase of a chicken. I couldn't cook at all. The only thing I could make was soup. I had never read a cookbook so I knew nothing about clarifying stocks or using egg yolks as thickeners.

I discovered the secret of how to make a dozen different soups quite by chance. One day I came home from school and decided to try my hand at what I'd seen my mother do many times. I started by sautéeing small pieces of carrot, onion and celery until they sizzled and started to brown. Then I poured on a jugful of stock, left the soup to simmer for half an hour, and proudly served it to my family.

The next evening, I did exactly the same thing but I added tomatoes and tomato purée and put the whole thing through a wonderful gadget called a mouli. It was used before the invention of food processors and was an easy way to pass the vegetables through a sieve. You pressed them down so that all that was left after the handle had been turned a few times were the fibrous remains, leaving a smooth and delicate purée in the bowl beneath. If there was no stock, I used milk or cream. Leeks and potatoes turned into vichyssoise. Celeriac had an earthy richness. That was it – chunky soup or smooth soup, but it tasted different every time.

My passion for soup making had one disadvantage. I convinced myself and my family that I could do nothing else. A few years later I left home to get married and since it was the custom then for wives to know how to cook, I realised that I would need to improve my reputation. I had been given a book called "Cookery in Colour". It was an encyclopaedia that explained everything from 'Apples, how to peel', to 'Zest, how to grate'.

I used it for our first dinner party and managed to produce a four-course meal consisting of grapefruit, soup (of course) and an over-cooked roast with frozen peas. The potatoes were that dreadful combination of being both underdone and burnt in places. The pièce de résistance was tinned pears with chestnut purée and a hot choco-late sauce.

The next day I took out another gift – a special book with heavy paper, bound in crimson leather and designed to record important occasions. On one side there was a table plan and on the other was space to write in The Guests, The Menu, The Wines and 'Gown and Jewels Worn'. I truthfully recorded the whole nerve-wracking occa-sion. The next few entries described experiments with fried potato balls and some veal chops that cost a week's salary. There was a space at the bottom of each page headed 'Comments'. I was desperately concerned with impressing the guests, as were most of our friends.

When I moved house there were leaks in the ceiling and packing cases everywhere. One of my neighbours was pretty and amusing so I invited her in for a cup of tea to cheer me up. We became good friends and later spent many happy evenings, mainly in my home. She never asked me to pop in for a coffee, but eventually planned an elaborate dinner with the most expensive ingredients. She told me then that she had been too nervous to reciprocate earlier because all her best china was at her parents' home abroad. The evening went off fine but I would have preferred a more relaxed friendship over the occasional cup of coffee in a plain mug.

Entertaining has always been a game of one-upmanship. Years ago women's magazines used to give instructions for a snazzy wine sauce to pour over the boss's coq au vin. Not much has changed. The women may be the bosses now but they still buy magazines. They read about models who are flown to the Seychelles to be photographed with a glimpse of designer beachwear and bowls of exciting seafood. The message is the same – something exotic is required to transform your Crouch End dining room into a Caribbean paradise, and since it's hardly possible to transform the weather, it has to be the food.

This may be the message of the ad men but it is a mistake. The way to get a good reputation is not to aim for a Michelin star, but to build up a repertoire of dishes which work. There is little time for trying recipes out beforehand, so an experimental dish often makes its first appearance at the dinner party table. This is why so many column inches are devoted to the once-a-year Christmas turkey. You can't afford to make a mistake with such an investment, and there is no way of trying it out the week before.

It's taken me a long time to discover that if you really are intent on impressing your guests, you will do far better to serve a plate of cool grilled vegetables, rather than keep dashing into the kitchen to stir a curdling hollandaise sauce. The leather-bound dinner book turned out to be the first in a continuous account of what I served to whom and what was wrong with it. The elegant volumes were replaced with ordinary lined notebooks. There was never a mention of what I wore, but increasing descriptions of the food and whether or not it worked. As the pile of books grew, I found myself using them as a diary, reflecting my thoughts on the events surrounding the meals. I wonder now how I coped with the night in 1972 when I wrote "they all enjoyed themselves. We had a power cut from 6 till 9 but heated the food later." Was I angry when I described "a dreadful evening. R was in a bad mood, complained about the whisky, the wine and the soup and refused the chocolate sauce which he's supposed to like"?

The style of cooking has changed very much. Everything seemed to be wrapped in pastry – swan vol-au-vents filled with mushrooms, salmon en croûte, stuffed chicken en croûte, even some little sticks filled with beef which I called 'mincemeat cigarettes'. That term would be unacceptable today – as would the mountains of whipped cream that I piped into profiteroles and coffee hazelnut gâteaux. Then came the years of nouvelle cuisine. I bought the obligatory octagonal white plates and served sauces under fanned out slithers of rare lamb or plaited fillets of brill and salmon. Every dessert was garnished with a sliced kiwi fruit – now so out of fashion that the poor farmers in New Zealand ha ve gone out of business.

Of course I am still concerned about my reputation and would be happy to think I have inherited my mother's good name. At the age of ninety one she still serves sandwiches without the crust for tea and would never dream of inviting anyone to her flat without offering them a home-made Danish pastry. Her grandchildren have a different approach. They come home from work and offer their friends a glass of wine, while they cook in front of them, amidst a mound of saucepans and a sink full of salad leaves. Here are some recipes that both generations would be proud of. The first three are unashamedly slow, needing time and patience. The rest are far quicker.

Chunky Beef and Vegetable Soup

Making soup calls for very little expertise, since there is no weighing of ingredients or exact timing. Once you can do it, you have mastered the first course of any meal. It's worth knowing how to make a meat stock, which is best done the day before. However, you can skip the instructions and make the soup with water and a cube, but it won't taste so good.

For the stock:

2 lbs	900g	meaty beef bones (for the stock)
2 large		onions
2 large		carrots
I head		celery
2		leeks
8 oz	225g	lean steak
I - 2 tbsp		oil
I½ pts	850ml	stock (or water and a beef cube)
		salt, pepper

You will need: a very large saucepan; a strainer; a large bowl.

Put the bones in the saucepan, cover with cold water and bring to the boil. Skim off the foam which will rise to the surface while it bubbles, cover the pan and simmer over low heat for an hour. Meanwhile wash all the vegetables and peel the onions and carrots.

Throw one onion, a carrot and some celery sticks into the stockpot and continue simmering for at least another hour, preferably two or three. Keep an eye on it to see that the liquid doesn't boil away and then strain it through a sieve into a large bowl. Leave the stock to cool. (If you refrigerate it overnight a layer of fat may appear on the surface and this is easier to remove once it is cold.)

Cut the meat into small dice. Peel and chop the remaining vegetables into small pieces. Heat the oil in the pan and over high heat, sauté the meat, turning it around until the pieces are no longer red. Add the vegetables and continue frying for a few minutes over medium heat. Pour over the water or stock and turn up the heat to bring the soup to the boil. After a few minutes take a large spoon and skim off the froth which will have come to the surface and discard it. Then lower the heat, put on the lid and leave the meat and vegetables to cook slowly for about an hour. Taste the soup adding pepper, a little salt and perhaps some more water.

Golden Gravy Chicken

The ingredients for this recipe are deceptively simple, unlike Coq au Vin, which needs a whole bottle of Beaujolais, garlic and herbs. I hardly dare to admit that I find that sour and watery and would prefer to have a glass of wine separately. This chicken, preferably a boiler not a roaster, cooks in its own rich gravy and is one of those rare dishes that is better made the day before and reheated, as the flavour improves overnight. The recipe will serve 5 – 6 people.

a 5 - 6 lb	2.5kg	free range chicken
2 tbsp		plain flour
		salt, pepper
½ tsp		paprika
I tbsp		oil
I pt	570ml	hot water

You will need: a large pot that can stand on the hob and go in the oven. Preheat the oven to 325F, 160C, Gas 3.

Pour the oil into the pot and set it over low heat. Make sure the chicken is quite dry and then lower it into the pot and turn it around as the oil starts to sizzle. Turn the heat up and brown the chicken on all sides, turning it frequently so that the wings, legs and breasts all come into contact with the base of the pan. Sprinkle over the flour, some salt, pepper and the paprika. Immediately pour on half the hot water and stir to make sure there are no lumps. Add the remaining water and bring it to the boil. Cover the pan and transfer it to the heated oven.

Cook the chicken for about an hour and a half. Turn it over and spoon over some of the gravy, adding a little more water if it has evaporated. (Gas and electric ovens behave differently and temperatures do not always remain constant.) Continue cooking the chicken until it is tender – about another hour and a half for a boiling chicken, or three quarters of an hour for a roaster.

When it is cooked the gravy will be thick and golden, but there will be a layer of transparent fat on the top. If you are serving it straight away, remove the fat with a large spoon. Alternatively pour the gravy into a deep bowl, leave it to cool and put it in the freezer until the fat turns to a pale, solid layer like ice on a pond. Then lift it off with a knife and pour the chilled gravy over the chicken. Refrigerate the dish overnight and reheat it gently on the hob until the gravy is bubbling and the chicken is heated through.

Slow Roasted Duck

It took me years to discover that the secret of tender meat under a crackly skin is long slow cooking. It's an easy dish because the potatoes and onions are cooked at the same time.

a 5 lb	2.25kg	duck
1 lb	450g	small onions
4 very large		potatoes
2 – 3 tbsp		oil

You will need: a baking tin; a rack; a skewer; a large, shallow ovenproof dish and a bowl.
Preheat the oven to 425F, 220C, Gas 7.

Prick the duck all over with the skewer, pressing it right into the flesh. The fat lies in a layer under the skin and pours out through these holes.

Peel the vegetables and cut the potatoes into small pieces. Spoon the oil into the ovenproof dish and put the potatoes in one side and the onions in the other. Shake it slightly and turn the vegetables over so that they are lightly coated. Put the dish on a lower shelf in the oven.

Put the duck on the rack, in the baking tin, and cook on a high shelf for about half an hour. Open the door, lift out the duck and pour any fat out into a bowl. Turn the oven down to *325F, 160C, Gas 3*, and replace the duck. Leave it to cook slowly for another hour, occasionally turning it over and pouring off any more fat which has accumulated at the bottom of the tin. Turn the potatoes and onions too, to make sure they are browning evenly. Then turn the heat back to high (*425F, 220C, Gas 7*) and continue roasting for the final half hour until the duck skin is crisp. Have ready a warm serving dish and plates. Cut the duck into quarters and surround with the roasted potatoes and onions.

Roast duck goes well with Apple Sauce (page 45) or Kumquat Preserve (page 183).

Winter Fruit Platter

This serves six on its own, or more with another dessert.

1	pineapple
6	seedless clementines
12	lychees

Cut the pineapple in half lengthwise, taking care not to cut off the green top. Cut each half again into three and remove the hard core in the centre. Arrange the pineapple segments around a large flat dish. Peel the clementines and cut them in half horizontally. Take the skins off the lychees. Arrange the clementines, cut side up, around the pineapple and scatter over the lychees.

Ricciarelli

These soft almond biscuits are a variation on a speciality from Siena which are usually diamond shaped.

1 tbsp		oil
3 oz	75g	flaked almonds
3 oz	75g	sugar
4 oz	100g	ground almonds
1		orange (zest only)
2		egg whites

You will need: a large flat baking tray; an egg whisk; 2 bowls and a grater. Preheat the oven to 250F, 120C, Gas ½.

First grease the tin with the oil. Chop the flaked almonds finely. (An easy way to do this is to put them in a plastic bag and crush them with a rolling pin). Stir in the sugar and ground almonds. Grate the rind of the orange and add this to the mixture. In another bowl whisk the egg whites until they are stiff. Gradually add some of the whisked whites to the nut mixture. It should be firm enough to form into small balls (it makes about 24). You won't need to use both the whites but it is hard to whisk as little as one egg white. Flatten the balls slightly and arrange them well apart on the tray. Bake the ricciarelli for 12 – 15 minutes. They swell slightly and seem soft when you take them out but harden a little as they cool. They can be stored in an airtight container and freeze well.

Courgette and Almond Soup

Whereas meat stocks improve with long slow cooking, vegetables and fish do not. Stocks made with either of these need only about half an hour for the flavour to infuse. Remember that a cube will taste stronger but saltier.

For the vegetable stock:

2		carrots
2		onions
4 or 5		mushrooms
I		leek (or 3 sticks celery)

For the soup:

I oz	25g	butter
I½ lbs	700g	courgettes
I pt	570ml	vegetable stock (or a vegetable cube and water)
½ pt	285ml	milk
		salt and pepper
2 oz	50g	ground almonds
2 oz	50g	toasted slivered almonds
2 fl oz	50ml	single cream or crème fraîche

You will need: a saucepan; a liquidizer or food processor and a strainer.

Wash and peel all the vegetables. For the stock, cut one onion, the carrots, mushrooms and leek into small chunks and put them in a pan. Pour over enough boiling water to cover and then simmer for about half an hour. Strain the liquid into a bowl and wash and dry the saucepan.

Cut the courgettes and the other onion into thin slices. Melt the butter in the saucepan and immediately throw in the vegetables. Stir them and sauté over high heat for a minute, then reduce the heat to avoid burning the butter. When the onion starts to colour very slightly pour on the vegetable stock. (You can use a vegetable cube dissolved in water instead, but it won't taste the same.) Season with salt and pepper, simmer for about twenty minutes and then stir in the ground almonds and the milk. Purée the soup in a liquidizer or food processor. Pour it back into the pan and reheat it gently but don't let it boil. Serve with a dollop of cream or crème fraîche in each bowl and decorate with a few toasted almonds.

Pasta with Asparagus and Nuts

To boil pasta you need a lot of water. What the Italians call 'al dente' means literally 'at the tooth', so it should have a bite and not be too soft. The cooking time on packets is a good guide, because different shapes require different times.

1½ lbs	675g	pasta (fusilli or penne)
1½ lbs	675g	thin asparagus spears
½ jar	140g	sun-dried tomatoes in oil
1 tsp		tomato purée
4oz	100g	toasted almonds
4oz	100g	parmesan cheese
		salt, black pepper

You will need: a very large saucepan; a smaller saucepan or the microwave; a small bowl; a strainer or colander and a cheese slice or vegetable parer.

Half fill the saucepan with water and bring it to the boil. Throw in a heaped teaspoon of salt. While it is boiling prepare the other ingredients. Wash the asparagus and cut off the stalks leaving the tips about 4 inches long. In a microwave dish arrange the asparagus spears in a single layer, sprinkle over 4 tablespoons of water and cook on **high** for about 6 minutes. Alternatively boil them in lightly salted water in a saucepan for slightly longer.

When the large pan of water is bubbling, throw in the pasta and stir it once to stop it sticking together. The water will immediately start to rise and will look white and frothy. Turn the heat lower and continue boiling for about 8 minutes or until it is just tender, but not soft and mushy.

Meanwhile, cut the dried tomatoes into strips and put them in a bowl with about 4 tablespoons of the oil from the jar. Stir in the tomato purée, some salt and pepper. Put the bowl in the microwave and heat on **high** for about a minute. Alternatively heat the mixture in the saucepan until the tomato has softened slightly and the oil is hot. Shave the parmesan cheese into thin slivers.

When the pasta is cooked, drain it through a colander and pour it back into the saucepan. Immediately toss in the hot tomato dressing and stir it quickly to combine the two. Gently fold in the asparagus spears. Transfer the pasta to a large heated dish and scatter the toasted almonds and shaved parmesan over it.

Barbecued Fresh Tuna

Preparing the fish a few hours in advance makes the flesh more tender. It is served with new potatoes and a red salad.

4 steaks		fresh tuna (about ¾" thick)
3 tbsp		olive oil
I tsp		balsamic vinegar
I		lemon
For the potatoes and salad:		
2 lbs	900g	very small new potatoes
6 leaves		fresh mint
I each		radicchio and oak leaf lettuce
I bunch		radishes
I		small red onion
6 tbsp		walnut oil
2 tbsp		red wine vinegar
½ tsp		French mustard
		salt, pepper

You will need: a large shallow dish; a grill pan with a rack, or a barbecue; and a saucepan.

Place the fish steaks in one layer in the dish and pour over the olive oil and balsamic vinegar. Cover and leave in the fridge until you are ready to cook. (This is called marinading and helps to tenderise fish or meat.)

Wash the new potatoes. Cover them with cold water and a little salt, bring to the boil and throw in the mint leaves. Cook over medium heat for ten to twelve minutes or until the potatoes are done. (A sharp knife should go easily into the centre.) Discard the wilted mint leaves, drain the potatoes and keep them warm. Take the fish out of the fridge.

Wash the salad, and dry the lettuces well. Arrange the leaves and radishes in a large bowl. Slice the onion very thinly and scatter over a few rings. Mix the oil, vinegar and seasonings together, and pour the dressing over the salad at the last minute.

To cook the fish, preheat the grill or barbecue until it is very hot. Brush the rack with a little oil. Lift the tuna out of the marinade and grill for two minutes on each side. This method of cooking fish meansthat it is just done – if y ou cook it much longer it becomes tough and leathery. Carefully lift the fish on to a heated platter and serve with wedges of lemon, the potatoes and tossed salad.

Apple Cheesecakes and Blackberry Sauce

It's generally not a good idea to bake in a microwave oven since most cakes need an appetising brown crust but cheesecake is the exception. Not only do these individual desserts work amazingly well, there is really no better way of making them, so for once there are no 'conventional' instructions. Serve the cheescakes on large individual plates with the sauce (called a 'coulis') on the side.

2 large		eating apples (preferably coxes)
9 oz	240g	fromage frais
4		eggs (4 yolks and 2 whites)
4 – 6 tbsp		vanilla sugar
2 flat tbsp		self raising flour
8 oz	225g	blackberries
3 - 4 tbsp		apricot jam
½		lemon

You will need: 6 plastic, china or glass ramekins 2 fl oz / 50ml size; a large bowl; a sieve and a pastry brush.

Peel and slice the apples thinly and arrange them in a single layer on a large plate. Cook on **high** for 1 – 2 minutes until they are soft. In a large bowl mix the fromage frais with 4 tablespoons of sugar. Whisk two whole eggs and two yolks together and add them to the soft cheese mixture, stirring vigorously to make it smooth. Sift the flour through a strainer and gently fold it in. Lift the mixture up and over until the flour has disappeared. Spoon the cheesecake mixture into the ramekins and arrange them around the outside of the turntable or a large plate. Cook on **low** (360W) for about 4 minutes. The mixture will rise and then fall again and is cooked when it no longer looks runny in the middle. (The timing may vary in ovens of different output, but it is important not to overcook the mixture as it becomes firmer as it cools.) When it is cold turn it out of the dishes. Run a knife around the edges and put a plate on top before turning them over.

Arrange the apple slices over the top of each cheesecake, overlapping them slightly and covering each cake completely. Put the jam on a plate and melt it on **high** for about a minute or until it starts to soften. Strain it through the sieve, stir in a squeeze of lemon juice and leave it to cool slightly. Brush the glaze all over the apple slices.

For the sauce, put 2 tablespoons of sugar and the blackberries in a dish. Cover and cook on **high** for 1 – 2 minutes or until the juices start to run. Press the berries through a sieve into a jug.

The Menus

Gratin Dauphinois

• • •

Goulash with Hamin Eggs

Fried Zucchini

• • •

Mango Ice

Chilled Pea Soup

• • •

Vegetable Crudités with Mayonnaise

Cheese and Almond Soufflé

• • •

Meringues and Chestnut Cream

The Techniques

Slow–cooking

Deep–fat frying

Making ices

Mayonnaise, Soufflés and Meringues

Those Wonderful Machines

There is an object that looks like two ladles made of mesh, fixed together so that one fits inside the other. It lies dormant in a basement cupboard, together with a dozen similar gadgets, that I use once a year. What is it for? If you want to make small potato baskets with grated potatoes fried in oil, this is the thing you will need.

I also have a gift from a Danish au pair – a heavy pan with round indentations called an apfelskiver. It was a skillet for some kind of apple pancake but the instructions have been lost, so there it sits, with the waffle iron and the pineapple cutter – gadgets that are rarely used because they have only one purpose in life.

If you are short of space or money you can manage with very few gadgets or machines. You may be surprised to discover that the recipes in this book have so far featured nearly all the basic techniques of cookery. The first chapter alone involved boiling, frying, roasting and steaming. The next pages covered baking, grilling and stewing. Yet till now I haven't mentioned kitchen tools or what the chefs call a 'batterie de cuisine'. In the early recipes there is no weighing or measuring and you can manage with a cup, a tablespoon and a teaspoon. A weighing machine is useful in baking where precision is important, but even there you can calculate the amounts you need from the markings on packets of butter or blocks of chocolate.

I've purposely delayed talking about implements because you can get started with the kind of equipment you might find in a rented kitchen – an oven with a grill, a hob, some plates and a few pots and pans. A chopping board helps to avoid making gashes in your table or work surface.

To do the work of basic food preparation you need five or six different items:
- a fork
- some spoons
- some sharp knives
- stacking ovenproof glass bowls
- a grater
- a sieve
- a non-stick frying pan

The fork can be used to whisk, a large enough sieve will double as a colander for straining, and the non-stick pan reduces the amount of oil in any dish that calls for frying.

For baking you need to add a flan tin with a removable base, a deep cake tin and a shallow baking tin. A spatula is useful for scooping out mixtures and a palette knife that bends is almost indispensable. To test if a cake is done requires a skewer, but you can manage quite well with a strand of hard raw spaghetti. You might also pick up a pastry brush next time you are in a kitchen department because it's more hygienic than the alternative, which is using your fingers.

To make the work easier, to attempt more complicated dishes and to tackle all the recipes in this book, you need to add just two electrical machines. What are they? I shall tell you later. Why only two? Because many of the machines sold in kitchen departments have serious drawbacks which the salesmen never divulge.

The Machines You Can Do Without

First there is the **food processor**. It certainly has its uses: slicing apples or potatoes, rubbing in fat and flour for pastry, and processing meat for hamburgers and mince. But all of these can be done by hand or by the butcher. It is only when you get the machine home that you discover the annoying side of this wonderful invention.

If you process mashed potato, it turns into glue; to cut cucumbers into even slices involves careful arrangement into the feed tube, otherwise you get uneven oval pieces. Anything sticky has to be scraped off the maddening tube in the centre. Worst of all is the slurp-slurping sound that comes if you are mixing too much liquid. It's quickly followed by the soup or sauce leaking round the edges. It then takes fifteen minutes to clean the machine and wash up all the beastly pieces.

The manuals that come with these machines never take the clearing up time into consideration. In a recipe for mushroom risotto, one suggestion is to start this way: "Peel the onion and cut it in half or to fit the feed tube. Fit the slicing disc and slice the onion." For this task a sharp knife and a cutting board would be far less trouble than yanking the bowl off the base and washing up four awkward shaped parts.

Slow-cookers also come with some misleading instructions. It is a common belief that you can throw in meat and raw vegetables and five hours later come home to a delicious stew. Firstly, slow-cookers really are slow – they barely simmer the food – so that if you put the meat in, cold, at 9 a.m. it may still be tough when you return at 5 p.m. Secondly they are not the one-pot miracle that is often claimed. The casserole will have a far better flavour if you start by browning the meat and some onions in a frying pan and then transfer them to the slow cooker. However, the advantage of really slow cooking is that with fifteen minutes' effort in the morning you can expect a rich, warming meal in the evening, and if you leave work an hour late you can be sure the food will not be dry or burnt.

Electric deep fat fryers are great. The oil is kept at a constant temperature so the food absorbs less fat. This also reduces the chance of starting a chip pan fire which is usually caused by overheating. Also, if you fry a fillet of fish and then some doughnuts, the flavour of the fish will not transfer to the sweet buns. But there is one disadvantage. A large fryer calls for many pints of oil and since it is recommended that oil should only be used three or four times, you have to consider the cost and difficulty of disposing of it. You can't put it down the sink and it's no fun pouring it back into the empty bottle. Most fish and chip shops don't seem to have this problem as a recent survey shows that many of them change their oil once a month and some even make it last a year.

If there is space on the worktop there are many more machines to fill it up: sandwich toasters, bread bakers, juicers, ice cream makers, espresso machines – they are all fun to own and play with but you need a large kitchen to accommodate them all.

The Two Machines You Really Need

I promised to tell you about the two electrical items that I think are essential. They both take up little space, are reasonably cheap and can be used for dozens of tasks.

The first is a **liquidizer**. It is hard work pressing food through a strainer and even harder work making mayonnaise by hand. A liquidizer will buzz up vegetables into a velvety soup and transform fruits into a juicy purée. It takes seconds to turn leeks and potatoes into vichyssoise and half a minute to make one of those sauces from strawberries or raspberries that smart chefs call a coulis. You can make milkshakes and baby food, crushed ice and apple sauce - all as smooth as the best food processor and far less lumpy than the worst, at a fraction of the cost.

The second machine you need is an **electric mixer**. A small hand-held one is fine since it will cope with the flour, butter, sugar and egg mixture of most cakes, will whisk egg whites for meringue and whip cream into peaks. It will mash potato and smooth out lumps in custard and best of all, it can be held over a saucepan to mix choux pastry or zabaglione. The large, stable giants that sit on the worktop can beat eggs and sugar for five minutes until the thick pale mixture is almost climbing out of the bowl. Not only can you go out of the kitchen and leave them to do the work – you have to, since the noise is deafening.

The purists believe a perfect mayonnaise should be beaten by hand and meringues are better using a copper bowl and a hand whisk. They are right of course. But cooking should be fun so most of us would prefer to avoid spending fifteen minutes on a boring task and use the time more productively.

It is easy to become a slave to the machines in the kitchen, believing that we are incapable of producing good food without them. A few small gadgets can sometimes be of more use than the newest electronic marvel. In a commercial bakery, a food consultant was working on some experimental savouries, testing recipes for a new line. There were industrial sized ovens and mixers but not a single small knife and when he needed to slice some onions, the only thing he could find was one with a ten inch blade. When a chef travels, the only thing he takes with him is a set of knives.

If I were going to cook somewhere else, there are two gadgets that I would take. Both of them are small and cheap. One is a vegetable parer – made of plastic or metal with a horizontal razor sharp blade. It whips the skin off potatoes, carrots or courgettes quite painlessly. The other is a self-cleaning garlic crusher. Why would you want one of these? Because garlic is good in ratatouille and crisp sauté potatoes but not so good all over your hands while you are cutting up fruit salad. The press pushes out tiny pieces of garlic leaving the skin behind, and with a quick flick, reverses to get rid of the tough bits you don't want.

Many good dishes were invented by accident – without machines. Steak was tenderised by cowboys who placed the meat under their saddles. The first roast pork was probably discovered after a fire in the barn where the pigs were kept. But these days it is only chefs with many assistants who are contemptuous of the machines that ordinary people rely on. They can't believe that a microwave oven, which can be used to puff up a packet of popcorn, can also make the best sole and salmon mousseline you can imagine. Learning to be in control and to get the best out of the machines is as important as realising that a computer can be used to word process a letter or to put a man on the moon.

The first menu uses machines you can manage without so it includes instructions for alternative methods. The second menu uses the two essential machines you need.

Gratin Dauphinois

The classic dish contained double cream but many people are concerned about fat. For a full, but not over rich flavour, I use ordinary milk – not skimmed, which is too far in the other direction.

1 lb 12oz	800g	potatoes (about 3 large ones)
		knob of butter
8 tbsp		grated gruyère cheese
3 tbsp		grated parmesan cheese
		salt, black pepper
½ pt	300ml	milk

You will need: a food processor with a slicing disc (or a sharp knife); the microwave or a small saucepan; a large gratin dish (a shallow ovenproof dish about 12" × 6" (30 × 15 cm).
Preheat the oven to 375F, 190C, Gas 5.

Cut the potatoes into very thin slices. Rub the butter all round the gratin dish, particularly up the sides and round the top edge. (This has nothing to do with the taste but is a precaution to help with the washing up since baked-on bits are hard to wash off.) Precook the potato slices very briefly either in a covered microwave dish on **high** for two minutes or in boiling water in a saucepan for the same time. Drain the potatoes and arrange the slices, slightly overlapping, on the base of the buttered dish. Sprinkle with salt (not too much), pepper and half the gruyère cheese. Repeat with another layer and add the remaining cheese and more seasoning. Use up the last few potatoes, cover with the grated parmesan cheese and pour over the milk. Bake for about 45 minutes or until the top is brown.

Goulash

The advantage of slow cooking is that it improves certain cuts of meat and you can go out for long periods while the flavour develops.

2		large onions
I lb I2oz	800g	braising beef, cut into thick slices
2 tbsp		flour
2 tsp		paprika
3 - 5 tbsp		oil
		salt
14 oz	400g	tin of tomatoes in juice

You will need: a non-stick frying pan; a slow cooker or a casserole dish and an oven.
Preheat the slow cooker on a high setting for about 10 minutes or the oven to 375F, 190C, Gas 5.

Peel the onions and cut them into thick slices. On a large plate, mix the flour, paprika and salt and press this mixture on to both sides of the beef. Dust off the excess, briefly heat half the oil in the frying pan and brown the meat until it is seared on both sides. Transfer it to the slow cooker (or the casserole dish). Throw the remaining seasoned flour into the frying pan with the rest of the oil and mix it into a paste. Stir in the tomatoes with the juice and an extra canful of boiling water. Season and mash the tomatoes slightly and keep stirring the sauce until it boils. Pour it over the beef and cover it with a lid. Turn the slow cooker control down to low and leave the goulash for five to eight hours. In the oven it will take two and a half to three.

Hamin Eggs

This is a favourite dish of observant oriental Jews who don't work or cook on the Sabbath. The eggs are cooked overnight in their shells and the texture changes from the toughness of an ordinary hard boiled egg to honey-coloured creaminess. They can be cooked alone or buried in the rich dark gravy of a beef casserole.

6	eggs
6	onions (skins only)
3 tbsp	oil

You will need: a slow cooker or a covered pot in the oven; a small saucepan. Preheat the slow cooker to low or the oven to 250F, 130C, Gas ½.

Cover the eggs with water and boil them for about five minutes. Pour away the water and wrap each egg, in its shell, in the washed onion skin. Arrange the wrapped eggs in the slow cooker (or a heavy casserole), add enough fresh water to cover them by about half an inch(1.2cm). P our in the oil and cook the hamin eggs for at least six hours (or overnight) on a very low setting.

To serve them, discard the onion skins and coloured water, shell the eggs and serve them warm as a starter with salad or with meat as a main course. (If you are cooking them with the goulash, simply immerse the unwrapped eggs in the gravy and leave out the onion skins and theoil.)

Fried Zucchini

The Italians have a marvellous way of cooking courgettes - or zucchini as they call them. For these crisp little sticks nothing but deep frying will do - any deep pan, lots of oil, (preferably green olive oil) but don't go away to answer the phone in the middle.

8	courgettes
3 – 4 tbsp	plain flour
	salt, pepper
	oil (see below)

You will need: an electric deep fat fryer with a basket filled with oil to a depth of about 2" (5cm), or a heavy pan; a metal slotted spoon or strainer.

Wash and dry the courgettes and trim off the ends. Cut them into sticks, about the width of a pencil and 3" (7.5cm) long. Heat the oil until it reaches a temperature of 375F, 190C. (You can tell when it is hot enough for frying if a piece of vegetable sizzles as it touches the oil.) Spoon some flour on to a plate and season it with plenty of salt and pepper. Toss the courgette sticks in the flour and then fry them in the basket of the deep fat fryer or just in the hot oil for about five minutes. They are done when they are crisp and light brown. Lift out the basket or remove the zucchini (they've changed their name now they are cooked!) with a slotted spoon or strainer. Drain them well on absorbent paper. Serve immediately before they go limp.

Mango Ice

A sorbet is a combination of frozen fruit and sugar. Chilling the purée without the usual sugar syrup makes it more like an Italian 'semifreddo' (half cold), but you have to take it out and eat it before it goes rock hard.

2	ripe mangos
1	large ripe nectarine
2 - 3 tbsp	sugar

You will need: a bowl; a liquidizer or food processor, or a sieve. An ice cream machine makes the best consistency but is not essential.

Peel the mango and the nectarine and cut the flesh off the stones. This is a bit harder with the mango since it is more fibrous and needs to be scraped off the flat core. Purée the fruit in a liquidizer or food processor or press it through a sieve. Add sugar to taste depending on the sweetness of the fruit. Spoon the purée into the bowl and freeze for about half an hour. Stir the icy edges into the softer centre and put it back for another hour, stirring again a few times if you can remember. It should be just frozen and soft enough to spoon out. Alternatively churn the mixture in an ice cream machine for about 20 minutes and then transfer it to the freezer. It will be ready to eat after about half an hour and will keep for up to two hours.

Chilled Pea Soup

It will taste better if you use fresh summer peas, but it will take a little longer to shell and cook them (probably a matter of half an hour altogether). Frozen peas will do, though the flavour is not quite the same.

2 ¼ lbs	1 kg	fresh peas in their pods or
1 lb	450g	frozen peas
10 - 12 sprigs		mint
1 tbsp		oil
4		fat spring onions
12 fl oz	350ml	vegetable stock (see page 62)
½ pt	300ml	milk
		salt and pepper

You will need: a liquidizer; a covered shallow pot for the microwave, or a small saucepan; a large saucepan and a bowl.

If you are using fresh peas shell them and put them in a pot with 7floz (200ml) w ater and half the mint. Cover and cook in the microwave on **high** for 7 – 9 minutes or slightly longer in a saucepan. Discard the mint.

Chop the spring onions into small pieces, heat the oil in the saucepan and sauté the onions briefly. Don't let them get brown. Add the cooked peas, or the frozen ones, with the vegetable stock, season and simmer for about ten minutes. Put the soup into the liquidizer with the milk and blend until it is very smooth. Check the seasoning, leave it to cool and serve it with a few fresh mint leaves floating on the top.

Vegetable Crudités with Mayonnaise

French crudités are raw vegetables which are usually put on the table before a meal starts. I've included some lightly cooked beans and would serve them as a side dish.

For the mayonnaise:

2		eggs (2 yolks and 1 white)
½ pt	285ml	oil (olive or sunflower)
2 tbsp		wine vinegar or lemon juice
		salt, pepper
¼ tsp		mustard
For the crudités:		
2		large carrots
1		celery
½ lb	225g	french beans
½ lb	225g	baby corn cobs

You will need: a liquidizer or an electric whisk; a shallow covered pan for the microwave, or a small saucepan.

For the mayonnaise, put the eggs in the liquidizer with the seasoning. Start the motor and very slowly pour in some of the oil in a thin stream. It is important to drizzle it, rather than pour it, at the beginning. After a minute or so, the sound will change from a sloshing to a kind of glug glug and you can continue pouring in the rest of the oil slightly faster. (Alternatively, whisk the eggs in a bowl and start adding the oil drop by drop. Keep whisking and then drizzle in the rest of the oil until the mayonnaise is thick.) Then add the vinegar or lemon juice and taste for seasoning.

Wash all the vegetables and cut the carrots and celery into sticks. Microwave the beans with 3 tablespoons of water, covered, on **high** for 4 – 5 minutes. (Alternatively throw them into a pan of boiling water and cook for about the same time.) Drain them and immediately pour over some cold water to refresh them and keep the colour bright.

Arrange the vegetables on a large dish with a pot of mayonnaise in the centre.

Cheese and Almond Soufflé

The mystique about soufflés has concentrated on the wrong bit. Making them is not hard. They consist of two basic parts, gently folded together: a thick sauce and a pile of egg whites which have been beaten up with a lot of air. What you do need is to get the quantities and cooking time right, and to make sure the guests are waiting for the soufflé and not the other way round. The china manufacturers have persuaded people to buy special dishes because the cooked soufflé is brought to the table, but you can make individual ones in bowls or ramekins. This amount will make four small servings.

I oz	25g	butter
3 tbsp		flour
5 fl oz	150ml	milk
3		eggs (3 whites and 2 yolks)
2 oz	50g	mature cheddar cheese
2 oz	50g	parmesan cheese
2 oz	50g	flaked almonds
		pepper (no salt)

You will need: 4 china or ovenproof glass dishes (8fl oz/225ml capacity); a small and a large glass bowl; a small saucepan (optional); a spatula and a whisk.
Preheat the oven to 375F, 190C, Gas 5.

Separate the eggs and keep one of the yolks for another use. Grate the cheeses on to separate plates. Grease the base and sides of the dishes and sprinkle over a little of the parmesan cheese.

To make the sauce part in the microwave, melt the butter in a bowl for about 20 seconds on **high**. Stir in the flour. Heat the milk in the bottle or a jug on **high** for about 40 seconds. Stir the milk in to the butter and flour mixture (which is called a roux – nothing to do with the Brothers Roux). Put it back and continue cooking on **high** for about a minute, stirring it halfway. It should now be thick enough to stand the spoon in it (in fact, if the spoon is not metal you can leave it in while it cooks).

Alternatively make this sauce in a pan over gentle heat. Melt the butter with the flour, stir in the milk and keep stirring until the sauce thickens. When you pour it out you may have to clean a burnt base, which is why I prefer the first method.

Stir all the cheddar and half the parmesan into the sauce. Make sure the large bowl is quite dry. Put in the whites and if there are any specks of yolk, scoop them out using the egg shell. (Whenever you are whisking whites separately it's important not to have any bits of yolk and not to use a greasy bowl.) As you whisk it will first turn to foam and will then whiten and become quite firm. The moment they are right is what is usually called 'stiff but not dry'. However, damp egg whites are never 'dry' so a better way of describing it may be when you can turn the bowl upside down and the whites only slide a very little,unlik e for meringues (in the next recipe), when the mixture stays where it is in spite of gravity.

With a spatula lift a little of the beaten whites on to the sauce and gently fold it in. Keep spooning out more of the whites until you have incorporated them all into the sauce but don't beat the mixture. If you do it the other way and throw the pile of heavy sauce into the whites it will deflate them immediately and the idea is to keep in as much air as possible.

Spoon the soufflé mixture into the dishes. It should be at least half an inch below the rim which is the space needed for it to rise. Sprinkle over the rest of the parmesan cheese and scatter over the flaked almonds. Put the soufflés in a low shelf, making sure there is nothing above to stop them rising. Cook them for 10 -12 minutes. At the end of this time they will have risen and browned on top. The inside will be slightly runny – which is how I like it – but if you loathe runny egg in any form, carry on for another minute or two. Everyone's oven performs differently so it is hard to be precise. This is why I'm suggesting that you start with a small quantity and time it carefully. The next time it will come out exactly as you want it.

Meringues

The easiest way to use up egg whites is to make meringues. The secret is to make the mixture completely stiff before it is baked. If you don't have a forcing bag, you can just use a spoon. The meringues will taste as good but won't look as if they've come from the local pâtisserie.

2		egg whites
4 oz	115g	sugar
1 - 2 tbsp		oil

You will need: a large baking tin; an electric whisk; a forcing bag with a wide nozzle; some paper cake cases; a palette knife; a rack or sheet of greaseproof paper or foil.
Preheat the oven to 250F, 120C, Gas ½.

Put the egg whites into a bowl and whisk them until they start to go frothy. Carry on until they get whiter and then slowly pour in the sugar, whisking all the time until the meringue gets thick and glossy. It is ready when you can turn the bowl upside down and the meringue doesn't fall out.

Grease the baking tin with oil. Spoon the mixture into the forcing bag and pipe out little mounds all over the tin, taking care not to put them too close together. Bake for about an hour and a half. Some people like them very solid but they are done when the base is hard, even if the inside is still slightly soft. Lift off the meringues with a palette knife and leave them to cool on a rack or paper.

When the meringues are cold, sandwich them together with whipped cream or the chestnut cream in the next recipe. Pipe some more cream over each pair of meringues and put them in paper cases. Store them in the fridge, uncovered, for not more than an hour before serving.

Chestnut Cream

This is a good filling for meringues and also for sponge cake.

3 tbsp		vanilla sugar (see below)
7 oz	200g	unsweetened chestnut purée (half a tin)
5 fl oz	150 ml	whipping cream
For the vanilla sugar:		
1 lb	450g	sugar
1		vanilla pod

You will need: an electric or hand whisk; a small saucepan and a forcing bag.

To make vanilla sugar, split the long black pod lengthwise with a sharp knife. Half fill a screw-top jar with some sugar. With the tip of the knife, scoop the black seeds from the inside of the pod into the sugar and mix it well. Press the empty pod down and cover with more sugar. The flavour will be noticeable immediately and will intensify after some hours. Top the jar up with extra sugar whenever you use it.

For the chestnut mixture, put 3 tablespoons of vanilla sugar in a very small pan with 3 tablespoons of water. Slowly bring it to the boil and cook for three or four minutes, until it has thickened into a syrup. Mix in the unsweetened chestnut purée, beating well, and leave to cool.

To whisk the cream, it helps to chill the bowl first. All cream (single or double) starts as a pouring consistency, but only whipping or double cream will begin to form a trail and then thicken as you whip in the air. When it is nearly ready it looks like wrinkles on a furrowed brow. Take care not to overwhip it, or it will separate into globules.

Fold half the cream into the chestnut mixture. Serve the chestnut purée sandwiched between meringues or sponge cakes, and pipe the rest of the cream over the top.

The Menu

Focaccia

Onions Monégasque

• • •

Quick Salmon and Vegetable Terrine

Aubergine Cannelloni with Fresh Tomato Sauce

• • •

Chocolate Mousse with Chocolate Leaves

Summer Peach Berries

Fresh Cherry Cake

Twirly Biscuits

The Techniques

Making bread

Chocolate mousse

Chocolate decorations

Cake baking

Is It Worth the Trouble?

When our sons were small – there were three of them then (the fourth was born after a gap of fourteen years) – we moved house to a place called Hatch End. It truly did seem the end of the world to me – brought up in London – and I told everyone that it was really Pinner. Both suburbs were seventeen miles from theatres and museums, but the centre of Pinner was an old village with a fourteenth century pub and a wine merchant who'd been there almost as long.

My husband Michael spent all his free time sanding down planks of wood and mitreing the edges to make bookshelves. He then decided to make louvred doors on the cupboards in the bedroom. Most sane people go to the local DIY and buy the doors but he cut every single slat himself and took a year and a half to complete the job. Some men take fright at the words 'knock-down' and wouldn't even want to assemble ready made furniture. He was different. He had decided the louvred doors were worth the trouble.

The art of cooking attracts similar enthusiasts. Some will go to any lengths to make a perfect dish while others think it is too much trouble to read the instructions on a frozen TV dinner. I began to cook professionally because it was how I liked to spend my time and I discovered that there were enough people who didn't enjoy it, to make it profitable.

I started a small catering business, called Spoones. I can't remember now why it had such strange spelling, but the best thing about the whole venture was some nicely designed cards I had printed, along with a list of seventy different dishes. Thinking about my incompetence and inexperience makes me shudder now since I lurched from one disaster to another in the early weeks. The first one came under the grandly titled 'International' section. The previous week I had delivered some savouries called borekas; triangles of wafer-thin filo pastry, well known in the Middle East. I was due to prepare a repeat order but on that day I had mislaid the crucial card in my stack of handwritten notes. I tried, in vain, to reproduce the spinach filling from memory but failed dismally. Not surprisingly, the customer refused to pay.

In spite of my early failures Spoones began to thrive and I found myself driving for miles to deliver the orders. I happily cooked all day but disliked the other aspects of the business. A rather random method of costing led me into difficulties: the price list was based on the cost of fresh produce in August, but I quite forgot that this would double in December. The worst part was collecting the money. At one very opulent house, I rang the front door bell, holding a beautifully decorated chocolate dessert. I was told to go 'round the side' – presumably to the tradesman's entrance. When 'madame' arrived, she looked at the dessert and to my horror, ran her finger through the piped rosettes of whipped cream and chocolate leaves. "It looks far too professional" she said. "I have to make my friends think I did it myself."

It would be surprising if an after-work cook had the time to play with chocolate leaves. But like that customer, most people are reluctant to admit that they haven't made the food they are serving and still have a desire to show that they have gone to some trouble.

This conflict has led manufacturers to produce unfinished dishes, so that the last part can be done at home. Part-baked French bread is well known but even sausage rolls now come in ready-to-assemble kits. The pastry sheets are rolled and cut and just need to be wrapped round the sausages. The few minutes' extra work is considered worth while for the added feeling of achievement.

People who don't cook often say they are too busy. This is probably true, but it might be more honest to admit that they'd actually prefer to spend their free time scuba diving or playing poker. Time-management experts have a solution to the whole problem. They tell us to concentrate on primary tasks. This means setting oneself a lifetime goal like becoming Prime Minister and forgetting about secondary tasks like ironing shirts and baking bread. Making lists and planning out the day helps to achieve the ideal of never wasting a minute. What the experts forget is that bread baking can be a calming activity; punching dough is more productive than shouting at a parking warden after a hard day.

Apart from the time question, there is another reason why people don't make things that take a lot of trouble. It's fiddly and messy. If you're one of those people with long painted nails who don't much like the feel of food, you won't want want to get stuck into rolling pastry and kneading bread. If you enjoy making sandcastles on the beach and handling wet clay, you'll enjoy it.

There are other tasks which should be avoided by the more fastidious. Tiny onions are beastly to prepare. Your eyes water just as much as with large ones and the process is the same for each one; removing the base and peeling off the skin. To make matters worse your hands finish up an ugly brown colour. The stain and the onion-smelling fingers can easily be dealt with. A spoonful of salt rubbed over them with a wedge of lemon will remove every trace. Why should you bother? Because the onions can be left bubbling away and then left to cool in a syrupy glaze.

Stoning cherries also calls for the salt and lemon finger-cleaning technique. It doesn't matter if you come across the odd stone in a fruit salad, but it's another thing cracking your teeth when you bite into a slice of cake. There are gadgets on the market that will stone one or two at a time, but the inventors have still not solved the problem of the juice that shoots out over your clean white shirt.

It always takes time to deal with single, small things. You may wonder why people stuff marrows and not french beans; it's not because the beans wouldn't taste good. Everyone has different views on where to draw the line. I think it's worth stoning cherries, but my cut-off point is removing grape pips with bent hairpins to keep the grape intact.

All the recipes in this chapter involve some trouble but are not difficult. The menu is for a buffet meal for at least six.

Focaccia

Focaccia is a very simple bread. It is like pizza dough and is fun and easy to bake. The bread is made with olive oil and before the dough is cooked it is flattened into large rounds. Then comes the fun part. You press the ends of your fingers in to make a pattern and fill up the holes with pieces of black olive or whatever else you fancy.

The process is foolproof and the result is a lot nicer than the plastic-wrapped slabs you can buy. Fresh yeast is sometimes hard to find. 1oz/25g is the equivalent of 4 tsp of the store-cupboard dried version used here.

14 oz	400g	strong white flour
½ sachet		quick acting dried yeast (1 tsp)
¼ tsp		salt
10 fl oz		warm water (3 fl oz boiling, 7 fl oz cold)
6 tbsp		olive oil (4 + 2 for brushing later)
2		sun–dried tomatoes
4 or 5		small stoned black olives
1 tbsp		sea salt crystals (optional)

You will need: a large bowl and a clean cloth (or paper towel); a large round baking tray (about 14" / 35cm) or two small flan tins (if you don't have either you can make it square) and a rack.

Mix the flour with the salt and the dried yeast. Add the cold water to the boiling water to make it lukewarm and stir this, with the olive oil, into the flour. Bread will never rise if you kill the yeast with water that is too hot so having the temperature right is important.

With your hands form the dough into a ball and then turn it on to a floured surface and start what is known as 'kneading'. This means pressing it with your thumbs and pulling it back towards you to make it easy to handle. The dough may be a little sticky, so add more flour to the board and your hands as you keep doing this. As it gets stiffer you will need to use the heel of your hands to get a smooth, elastic ball.

After about five or ten minutes put the dough into a large oiled bowl and leave it, covered with a clean towel, to rise in a warm place. This will take between one and three hours, depending on the heat of the room, the weather etc. When it has doubled in size it will look very light but as soon as you take it out of the bowl, it will deflate. Knead it again very briefly. This is called 'punching it down'.

Oil the tin and press the dough right to the edges, making sure it is about half an inch thick (1.5 cm) and level. Then press your fingers into the focaccia at intervals making small holes. Cut the dried tomatoes and olives into small pieces and put these in the holes. Leave the bread to rise again. It will take about half an hour. After fifteen minutes, put the oven on.

Preheat the oven to 425F, 220C, Gas 7.

Bake the focaccia for 20 minutes. Take it out and brush over the remaining olive oil and sprinkle with sea salt crystals, if you like a salty taste. Leave to cool on the rack.

Onions Monégasque

These go well with cold meat or fish and can even be served on their own, as a starter.

1 lb	450g	small onions
10 fl oz	300ml	wine (red or white)
3 fl oz	80ml	olive oil
1 tbsp		wine vinegar (also red or white)
		salt, pepper
2 tbsp		tomato purée
4 oz	125g	sultanas (optional)

You will need: a bowl and a small saucepan.

Put the onions into a bowl and pour over some boiling water. Leave for a few minutes and then lift them out with a spoon. Peel the onions, preferably near a running tap as the water helps to stop your eyes watering. Put them in the saucepan and cover with the wine, oil, vinegar and seasoning. Cook over high heat until the liquid boils and then cover the pan and simmer until the onions are tender (about half an hour). Stir in the tomato purée and the sultanas, cook for another five minutes and then leave to cool.

Quick Salmon and Vegetable Terrine

A terrine is a slowly cooked rough pâté of fish or meat which is left to cool. A far quicker idea, with a pretty result, is to arrange flaked salmon around a small circle of spinach and to enclose it all in strips of courgette. It sounds much harder than it is.

1¼ lbs	575g	salmon fillet or steaks
4 tbsp		white wine
8 tbsp		mayonnaise plus more for serving
1½ lbs	675g	fresh spinach
2		very large courgettes
		salt, pepper
a few sprigs		fresh dill

You will need: a large dish with a lid for the microwave, or a saucepan large enough to take the fish in one layer, and a vegetable parer or sharp knife.

In the microwave cook the fish on **high**, sprinkled with the wine and covered with a vented lid (or clingfilm with a few holes to let the air escape). It will take 3 – 4 minutes and the fish is done when it is pale pink and opaque all over. Alternatively poach the fish in a pan with the wine and enough water to cover. Bring the liquid to the boil and simmer for about five minutes. Leave the fish to cool in the liquid to complete the cooking.

Wash the spinach very well and cook it, with no water, until it wilts, 2 – 3 minutes in a covered pot on **high** in the microwave or in a saucepan over low heat for a bit longer. Drain it very well, season with salt and pepper and chop it finely.

Wash the courgettes but don't peel them. With a vegetable parer or a very sharp knife cut them into long thin strips about an inch (2.5cm) wide . Cook them very briefly (this is called blanching) so that they will bend but are still slightly crisp. Do this in the microwave by arranging the strips on a large plate and cooking on **high** for about one minute. Alternatively throw them into some boiling water for about the same time and then drain. Leave them to cool.

Lift the cooked salmon out of the liquid and flake it with a fork. Mix it with half the mayonnaise.

To assemble the dish, pile the spinach in the centre of a flat dish. Spoon the salmon mixture round the spinach. Then, holding each courgette strip vertically, drape it round the salmon, overlapping where necessary, to make a circle. Decorate the round terrine with some sprigs of dill and serve the rest of the mayonnaise separately.

Aubergine Cannelloni and Fresh Tomato Sauce

There are two ways to bring out the moisture and any bitter juices in an aubergine. One is to salt the slices and leave them for half an hour, the other is simply to microwave them.

I lb	500g	aubergines (about 2 medium sized)
3 – 4 tbsp		olive oil
5 oz	175g	ricotta cheese
3 oz	75g	crème fraîche
3 tbsp		chopped herbs (mixture of chives, chervil, dill)
5 or 6		sundried tomatoes (optional)
For the tomato sauce:		
8		large tomatoes
I fat or 2 small		garlic cloves
		salt, pepper
pinch		sugar

You will need: a grill; a sheet of foil; a microwave dish or a small saucepan and paper towels.

Wash the aubergines and cut them into thin oval slices. Arrange the slices on paper towels and microwave in two batches on **high** for 3 minutes. Alternatively, salt them as above, and then rinse. Dry them well.

Preheat the grill to high.

Spread the oil over the foil and arrange the slices in a single layer, turning them over so that the oiled side is uppermost. Grill them for about five minutes to brown both sides. If necessary brush over a little more oil. Don't go away while they are grilling because it is easy for the edges to burn and you may need to move them around so that the hottest part of the grill reaches all the slices. Leave the aubergines to cool.

Cut the tomatoes and the garlic cloves in half and arrange in a shallow dish, sprinkle over two tablespoons of oil, cover and micro-wave on **high** for 3 – 4 minutes, or until the tomatoes are very soft. Alternatively, simmer them with several tablespoons of water as well as the oil, in a saucepan. Press the tomato mixture through a sieve, season with salt, pepper and a little sugar and leave to cool.

Mix the ricotta with the crème fraîche and the finely chopped herbs. Spoon a little of the cool cheese mixture on to each slice of aubergine, roll it up and arrange the rolls on a large dish. Serve with the fresh tomatosauce and, if y ou like, slices of sundried tomatoes.

Chocolate Mousse with Chocolate Leaves

The strange thing about this dessert is that the well-known mousse recipe is harder than the masterchef-style decoration of leaves and spirals on the top. If you've already tried making a soufflé, you'll have no problem folding in the egg whites to make it light.

For the mousse:

6		large eggs
6oz	175g	plain chocolate

For the chocolate decorations:

3 oz	85g	plain chocolate
12		small rose leaves

You will need: the microwave or a small saucepan; a large bowl and a small bowl; 2 large sheets of foil; a pastry brush; a whisk and an icing tube with a fine nozzle.

First make the mousse. Break the chocolate into small pieces. The best way to melt it is on a plate, uncovered, in the microwave for about two and a half minutes on **high**. Alternatively, put the chocolate into a bowl, set over a pan of simmering water, and stir gently until it softens. Separate the eggs and put the whites in a bowl. Mix the yolks into the melted chocolate, stir vigorously and leave the mixture to cool slightly. In the other bowl, whisk the egg whites until they are very stiff. Then gently fold the two together. To do this, start by taking a cupful of the whites and fold this slowly into the chocolate. Gradually add the rest, lifting the mixture from the bottom of the bowl. Take care not to beat it too much because the air in the whisked whites makes the mousse light. You just need to keep folding until there are no more white blobs. Spoon the mousse into a glass bowl and chill it for a few hours.

To make the decorations, first wash the rose leaves and dry them well. Lay the foil sheets on to two large plates. Melt the chocolate (this amount will take less time – about one minute) and then with the brush, carefully paint the back of each leaf, taking care not to get the chocolate on the other side or on the stem. Arrange the leaves, chocolate side up, on the foil and put them in the freezer.

To make the spirals, spoon any remaining melted chocolate into the icing tube (reheating it first on **high** for 20 seconds if it has gone hard). Then tak e the second plate and foil and pipe small spirals, starting at the centre and working outwards. The chocolate will flow very freely so keep your finger over the nozzle when you have completed each one. Place this plate in the freezer too. After about 15 minutes the chocolate will have hardened. To remove the spirals, just press gently underneath the foil and slide them off into a small container. For the leaves, holding the stem, peel off each leaf and arrange the chocolate leaves on a plate. Store the spirals and leaves in the fridge or freezer until the mousse is set and then arrange them over the top.

To freeze: Wrap the completed mousse and the decorations separately. To serve from frozen: Defrost the mousse in the fridge overnight or for several hours in a cool room. Decorate with the frozen leaves or spirals just before serving.

Summer Peach Berries

You could just arrange a platter of fruit. With a little more effort you can intensify the wonderful smell of fresh strawberries by buzzing them into a purée. The peaches hidden underneath won't discolour so you can make this dessert in advance.

1 lb	450g	strawberries
4		large ripe peaches
2 – 3 tbsp		sugar (optional)

You will need: a liquidizer or food processor and a bowl.

Put the strawberries into the bowl of a liquidizer or food processor. Switch on and process them briefly until they are puréed and there are no lumps. If you like stir in a little sugar. Pour the red purée into a glass dish.

Cover two of the peaches with boiling water and count to twenty. Take them out and slip off the skins with a knife. (If this doesn't work it means they aren't ripe.) Do the same with the other two and then slice the peaches straight into the strawberry purée and discard the stones.Push them down gently so that they are completely submerged. Cover the bowl and refrigerate for a few hours (even overnight).

Fresh Cherry Cake

This cake should be eaten on the same day as it doesn't keep as well as the old English version with sugary glacé cherries. Photographs of the perfect cherry cake always show the fruit suspended in the centre. The truth is, it doesn't matter if they stay on the top or sink to the bottom – it still tastes good. The method (called Victoria sandwich) is simple and if you are attempting a home-made cake for the first time, it's a good one to try.

8 oz	225g	cherries
6 oz	170g	self raising flour
1 tsp		baking powder
6 oz	170g	unsalted butter
4 oz	115g	sugar
3		eggs

You will need: a bowl; a strainer; a spoon or an electric mixer; a loaf tin 8"×3" ×3" (20cm × 8cm × 8cm), or a shallower cake tin about 10"×7" ×1" (25cm × 18cm × 3cm); greaseproof paper; a skewer, a long cocktail stick or a strand of spaghetti.

Prepare the tin by lining it with greaseproof paper. Put oil or butter on both sides, on the bottom to keep the paper down and on the top to stop the cake mixture sticking. Stone the cherries. Sift the flour and baking powder through a strainer. (This makes it lighter.)
Preheat the oven to 350F, 180C, Gas 4.

Beat together the butter and the sugar and then add one egg. (Always break each egg into a cup first, just in case one of them happens to be bad.) The mixture will now look sloppy. Keep beating and add the remaining eggs, one at a time. It may now look a bit curdled but add some of the flour, stir it well and it will begin to look like a batter. Quickly beat in the rest of the flour and as soon as it is smooth, stir in the stoned cherries. Spoon the mixture into the loaf tin, levelling off the top with a knife. Bake in the centre of the oven for about 40 minutes. A deep cake will take longer than a shallower one. To find out if the cake is done, you need to insert a skewer or cocktail stick right through the middle. If it comes out dry, the cake is cooked, if it is at all sticky, it needs another five minutes or so. Try not to open the door of the oven for the first half hour because the cake will sink if the mixture has not had time to set.

To freeze: Wrap the cooled cherry cake in foil or clingfilm. Defrost it at room temperature for several hours.

Twirly Biscuits

This might be seen as a time-wasting recipe if you have your mind set on furthering your career. However, if you have any pastry trimmings left after making a pie, it's a good way to use them up. The biscuits freeze well and are good with tea or coffee. As the basic pastry is unsweetened you need to add sugar.

8 oz	225g	pastry (half the quantity on page 36)
½ cup		vanilla sugar (see page 81)

You will need: a baking sheet or tin; a palette knife; a rolling pin.
Preheat the oven to 425F, 220C, Gas 7.

Sprinkle a little sugar (instead of the more usual flour) on to the worksurface and roll out the pastry into a neat rectangle. Sprinkle over a few tablespoons of flavoured sugar and using the palette knife fold the left hand edge over towards the centre. Fold over the right hand edge to meet it in the middle. Sprinkle some more sugar over this double thickness of pastry and then fold it in half again sideways, making four layers. Roll the pin over it again to make it thinner (about quarter of an inch thick). Then cut it across into strips the width of a pencil. Holding each end of the strip twist it into a spiral and lay the biscuits on an ungreased baking sheet. You may need to press the ends down to stop them unrolling. Bake for about 10 – 14 minutes, when they should look light brown. Take care not to burn them because the sugar helps them to cook fast.

Immediately they are done, slide the palette knife underneath to loosen them from the tin, otherwise they may stick. Wait until they are cool and store in a covered container or leave them out on a plate. If you do this you may find they have all gone by the time you are ready to put them away.

Take a Break

"I have a problem with food, with cooking food. I can't do it. It's too difficult. Too messy and too time-consuming. When I try it, it gets me down. I get angry and irritable. I get frustrated and depressed. I get hungry". This is a quotation from an article by a journalist called Jim Shelley, complaining that cookery programmes and books don't encourage or inspire him.

The previous chapter is full of dishes which, at first sight, might have terrified Jim Shelley. I imagine that you too have rejected a few recipes because they look hard, and others because they simply don't appeal to your taste. Yet I'm sure you have come a long way from the first hesitant dishes in the early chapters where you started to put together a few ingredients. You must have discovered how easy it is to fry, roast and steam. Even if you're not that confident with pastry or pancakes – it would be surprising if a few attempts turned out perfect results – I hope you've been encouraged to keep reading. If something hasn't worked – forget it. There's no exam at the end and you may find that you're better at some techniques than others.

It may be a good idea to stop for a while and have a breather. By now you may well have more enthusiasm and equipment than you started with. For the moment you may also have less cash since it costs money to buy even the limited tools that I've suggested. To balance this, your attitude to eating in restaurants may change as you discover that the dishes you were ordering are not that hard to make.

Of course there will have been failures. The next chapter should make you feel a lot better. If that doesn't, carry on and make yourself some comforting food from the one after that, or you could start putting together some menus of your own, using recipes which have gone down well.

At the beginning of the book you probably felt uneasy about inviting your friends to a meal. With so many techniques behind you, I'm sure you are finding the prospect of that dreaded word "entertaining" less worrying. The final few chapters should be a great boost for your morale. A hesitant cook is about to turn into an amateur chef.

Now that you have reached the half-way stage, here are a few comments about the recipes:

- The dishes don't necessarily need to be cooked in the order they come in the menu. For example, a cold dessert can be made early so that it's out of the way before you start to grill fish or microwave the vegetables.

- Some recipes are much longer than others. This doesn't necessarily mean that the tasks will take longer, but it does indicate that a new technique is involved which requires some explanation.

- In the early chapters I was quite vague with measurements and quantities, now I am being more precise. Especially with liquid mixtures, the size of a container can affect the cooking time and the end result.

- There is a discrepancy in the metric and imperial measurements. Since I prefer to work with the old method (not decimal) I have not always converted the measurements precisely. Where the exact amount is not crucial, for example with vegetables, I have taken an ounce to be 25g; where it is important to get the proportions exact I have used the more precise 28g. You should follow either one set of measurements or the other, especially with cakes and desserts where the division of fat, flour and sugar becomes far more important.

- You may find that the timing given for microwave instructions is not quite enough. As I mentioned earlier I use a powerful micro-wave with a 750W output. If yours is 650 or lower you may need to add on seconds or, in some cases even minutes. Ordinary ovens too may vary so that one with an efficient fan will cook faster or more evenly than one without. So don't be surprised if you need to make slight adjustments to adapt to your own equipment.

The Menus

Chicken Soup

. . .

Lamb Casserole

. . .

Lemon Soufflé

Stuffed Dates in Caramel

Italian Bean Salad

Tagliatelle with Cream and Parmesan

Roasted Sea Bass

Queen of Sheba Cake

The Techniques

Making a clear soup

Caramel

Roasting a whole fish

Disasters

There was once a beautiful Persian cat that adored salmon. One day it jumped on to the kitchen table to find an exquisitely decorated whole pink fish. It was irresistible. The cat started licking the tail and took a few small bites out of one side. At that moment there was a noise, so it jumped down and ran out into the garden. When the owner of the cat realised what had happened, she quickly cut round the fish that had been eaten and covered the gap in the salmon with some extra mayonnaise and a few more cucumber slices. The guests arrived and were served with the first course. Then they ate the salmon. It was a hot day, so when the woman came back into the kitchen she opened the back door for some air. To her horror, there was the cat, lying dead on the doorstep. Seeing what had happened to the animal, she agonised over what to tell her friends. Eventually she decided to tell the truth and suggested that they should all go to hospital. If they were in the first stages of poisoning it was vital to remove the contents of their stomachs.

After a miserable evening everyone went home. When the woman got back, she went to put out the rubbish and remembered the poor dead cat. She picked it up and there, on the doorstep under the cat's body, was a note saying: "Sorry, your cat was run over by my car – I shall contact you tomorrow".

I have been assured that this is a true story – it comes direct from the person who knew someone whose brother was the doctor who attended one of the guests who was at the dinner party!

During a lifetime everyone has disasters. Actors forget their lines. Hairdressers give perms that make your hair fall out. The only consolation is that experience does help to cover up some of the catastrophes.

There can't be a worse calamity when you are entertaining than to have no food at all. This happened one day when I had been married a very short time. We had invited a friend to dinner and I had arranged for the butcher to deliver the meat while I was at work. In those days people were more honest and it was perfectly all right to leave a package by the front door of a suburban house. I had planned to serve tomato soup, grilled chops and fruit salad – the only things I felt confident about. When I arrived home at 6 o'clock, to my horror, there was no meat and all the shops were closed. In desperation I phoned my mother, who calmed me down and told me not to panic. Half an hour later, she appeared on the doorstep with a lamb casserole, complete with vegetables and warm from the oven. Our guest arrived and I served it up. He was very impressed. "Well", he said "I must say you cook just like your mother". Looking back, I never thought to ask what my parents ate for dinner that night.

When things go wrong, it's sometimes possible to blame someone else. I had a good try on the occasion of my next blunder. Entertaining time again – and this time it was to be a friend who was coming to discuss some work with Michael. "Bring your girlfriend and she can talk to my wife," he suggested. "Come about 8.30". Well, to us that meant after dinner and in the 1960s that kind of entertaining meant coffee and cakes. I had progressed from my repertoire of three dishes and had learned how to make a very light sponge cake with the aid of an electric mixer. Every cake was a variation on the same theme – sponge cake with cream and jam, sponge cake with strawberries, chocolate sponge cake with cream, jam and strawberries. The guests arrived – bearing a bottle of premier cru claret. My husband chatted cheerfully while I brought on the coffee and cakes. I have never seen two people eat so much cake, so ravenously, but far from being proud of myself I was overcome with guilt, for I realised then that they were expecting a full dinner. When they had gone, I blamed my husband – for not explaining to them that we meant 'after dinner'. Only then did he begin to wonder why we had received such a nice bottle of wine.

I don't pretend that the years between the failures and the successes were trouble free. I was busy bringing up three boys and starting my catering business. By now it had expanded from one-off dinner party orders to much larger celebrations.

Worries about poisoning the guests (or cats!) must figure in every caterer's nightmares. I used to get very nervous before a big event as it was a great responsibility to produce massive quantities of food single-handed. The day after one of these parties my brother telephoned in a very agitated state. "Have you heard?" he asked. "Heard what?" I replied. "They are all ill, all 90 of them."

My mind fast-forwarded through the menu, trying to isolate whether it was the cold meats, the mayonnaise or the coffee mousse that had stricken the guests. By this time my brother was laughing and enjoying his joke. It took me a little while to recover from it.

A few days later I was to deliver a single order of a large birthday cake. Not an iced concoction with a firm layer of marzipan and fondant but another version of the famous sponge cake. This time it was so large it would only just fit in the fridge. Inside the layers was freshly whipped cream and a silky crème pâtissière flavoured with real vanilla – it even had the little black dots to prove it. The whole cake was soaked in Tia Maria and the top was decorated with chocolate coffee beans, more whirls of cream, and the best dark chocolate shaved into long, elegant curls. I had no box big enough to take this masterpiece so I had assembled it on a vast tray. I got the car out, ready to drive the ten minutes to the customer, and asked one of my sons to fetch the cake and sit and hold it during the short journey. Suddenly I heard an agonizing "Aaarrgh" from the kitchen. "I've dropped the cake" he groaned. As I rushed in I found all three boys convulsed with laughter as I had, once more, been taken in.

I really did drop a cake once but this one was frozen. Of course I couldn't run the business on my own without a freezer and much of the food that was ordered was prepared in advance and stored until the delivery day. It's well known that if a piece of buttered bread falls off a plate, the butter side hits the floor. It was the same with this cake. It was just like the one with the whirls and chocolate curls. The only difference was that it was taking up a whole shelf of the freezer, waiting to be packed away in a large box. I took it out and somehow it slipped out of my hands and fell. As it reached the floor the whole top flattened and crumbled. Fortunately the party was a week away but I was too desolate to start the whole thing again. Michael came from the garage with a saw and managed to saw off the whole of the crushed top, so all I had to do was start again with another pint of whipped cream to repair the surface damage.

By this time I was beginning to wonder if I was in the wrong job. I gave up catering – had a brief spell of giving private cookery courses and then began to write down some of the recipes I'd worked out over the years. Eventually I succeeded in convincing a publisher that the collection would form a book. I was taken out to lunch to discuss it, but I was so nervous negotiating the contract, that I couldn't enjoy a single mouthful.

It is even harder to do business at home. I had been working on some articles for a large magazine and invited a few of the editors to dinner in the hope that the series might continue and I would get more work. I spent the afternoon preparing an elaborate meal but when it was served everyone was busy talking and hardly noticed what they were eating. The following week I opened the magazine to look at the food page and discovered that they had a piece on edible gold food. No wonder they were unimpressed with what I had offered them.

The more skilled you become, the more people expect. Cooking for fellow food writers is a challenge. On one occasion I invited two of them to dinner. I pondered over the menu for days and finally devised what I hoped would be an elegant starter. It was a vegetable terrine, with pretty layers of french beans, baby corn cobs and spinach in between a delicate chicken mousse. Half an hour before the meal I went to turn out the terrine, to discover, to my horror, that the mousse was slightly soft and could never be sliced. I suddenly thought of the solution. I spooned the mousse on to large individual plates (giant plates make any food look better) and cut the vegetables and embedded them decoratively into each portion. Then I wrapped some long thin strips of courgette round each one. The colour contrasts looked good and no-one guessed at the panic that had taken place before the guests arrived. (Incidentally this near disaster was the origin of the salmon and courgette recipe in the last chapter).

I wasn't always so lucky in correcting my mistakes. Stuffed dates are a favourite sweet for Jewish festivals. The stones are removed and the dates are filled with marzipan and then each one is dipped in boiling caramel. The caramel sets in a thin, crisp layer and the dates look wonderfully glossy. I made them once, in a hurry, and although the caramel looked pale, I thought it would be fine and quickly used it to dip a whole tray of stuffed dates. After dinner I served them up. As I handed round the coffee I could see everyone struggling to disentangle something from their mouths. Stuck to their teeth was a sticky, sugary mess of undercooked caramel.

The next disaster happened to a good friend of mine. The subject of this one was a topic of many jokes: the famous Jewish chicken soup. (Here's one about two men in a market. One of them was buying chicken for soup. "How come this chicken has only one leg?" he asked. The stallholder replied: "It was in a fight". The man thought for a moment and then said: "Nu, bring me the winner".)

To carry on with the story, to make chicken soup you need an enormous, aged, boiling fowl. Not a delicate little poussin or even an ordinary, run of the mill, roasting bird. You also need a huge pan and patience. Chicken soup takes at least three hours to make. You can go out while it is simmering and when you come back there will be a powerful, savoury smell all over the house. As you lift the chicken out of the pan, the thighs will be heavy where the soup has collected under the skin and the flesh will be so soft it almost collapses off the bones. A layer of golden fat will form droplets on the top.

Most Jewish mothers make this soup about once a week – and for large families or many guests this means a giant pan. My friend was entertaining a large crowd for dinner on Friday night (the definitive 'chicken soup' night). For many of the guests it was their first visit to her home. The meal was carefully planned and the table was laid with the best silver and starched white linen. Everyone was waiting. She brought in an enormous tureen full of steaming chicken soup, and set it down on a little serving table. At that moment, the table collapsed and as it went down, so did a cascade of golden soup and slippery noodles. The carpet took on a faint orange tinge and the family surged forward to help mop up the liquid that hadn't already seeped into the floor below. Imagine the silence, the embarrassment – to say nothing of the half hour wait till the next course was ready.

It's not only formal occasions that can turn into disasters. Not long ago, we had invited a Swedish friend to supper – a relaxed meal in the kitchen. For dessert I had made a lemon soufflé that could be prepared ahead and would take exactly eighteen minutes to cook. After the main course, I popped the soufflé into the oven and served a large bowl of winter salad. We then embarked on an animated political discussion and our friend stopped eating to make his points. The timer was ticking on and I knew that in four minutes the soufflé would be ruined. I couldn't tell him to hurry (though perhaps that is what I should have done) and ten minutes later, as I cleared away the salad plates, the beautifully risen puff of lemon had turned into a heavy, overcooked pudding. I've learned from that experience that a cold dessert would have been simpler and today I would probably choose the scrumptious Queen of Sheba cake.

Some things that go wrong can be put down to inexperience. I suppose now I am more wary and try to avoid trouble before it happens. Planning for a possible emergency is better than trying to deal with one. Like insurance, it costs money, but it's a good idea to buy an extra avocado in case one turns out to be black when you cut it open, or to have ready a juicy melon and some blueberries in case the experimental pudding doesn't work.

Entertaining friends with special diets or allergies presents a different challenge. A guest who is allergic to peanuts will always explain in advance that a single nut could render him unconscious, but occasionally people can be less communicative. I remember an evening when I was serving roast veal to a crowd of young students. As I was about to plunge the carving knife into the meat, one of them said: "I'm awfully sorry – I'm a vegetarian." He was probably too embarrassed to mention it earlier, but I would have preferred even a ten minute warning so that I could have produced a bean salad or a plate of pasta.

The worst occasion I ever described in my leather-bound books was this one. A disaster not on a small scale, but a total evening-wrecker. We had invited two couples for dinner. On the day I was preoccupied and busy but that did not stop me trying to concoct a dish I had seen in a magazine. It was called "Mousseline de deux saumons" and featured both fresh and pickled salmon. The idea was to pound the fresh salmon with cream and cover it with a thin layer of gravlax, forming it into a shallow ring decorated with sprigs of fresh dill. I served a wedge to each guest and everyone seemed happy. Five minutes later one of my friends went very quiet, whispered that she had a fish bone caught in her throat and left the room. Almost immediately her partner jumped up and seconds later, they were roaring away in their car with my husband driving, on their way to the nearest casualty department.

I was overcome with guilt and embarrassment since I had remembered that there were bones in the salmon and in my haste I must have missed a few and buzzed them up in the food processor with the fish and the cream. The one that got stuck must have been as sharp as a razor because the visit to the hospital took up the whole evening. I was left, in silent misery, trying to make conversation with the remaining two guests, waiting for the return of the other three. They came back hours later. The fish bone had finally been dislodged by probes, x-rays had been taken and the patient was declared unharmed. That evening, however, still sticks in my memory.

The first menu in this chapter is a reminder of some of the disasters, which will hopefully not happen to you. The second one includes dishes to save the day, should things go wrong.

Chicken Soup

The consommé, which serves 6 – 8, is best made the day before. The result will be a broth that is golden, fragrant and robust – a million years away from what passes for stock from an oversalted cube.

6½ lb	3kg	boiling chicken, including giblets but not liver
2		onions
2		carrots
5		sticks celery
35 fl oz	I litre	cold water
		salt, pepper
a handful		fine vermicelli (called lockshen)

You will need: a very large saucepan with a lid; a large bowl or container; a strainer and plenty of time.

Wash the chicken very well and remove the parcel of giblets which is often packed inside. Put the chicken and the giblets into the pan. Add the vegetables and the water and bring it to the boil over high heat. As it boils, a white froth will come to the surface. Spoon it off into a bowl and throw it away. Add the seasoning (not too much salt), turn down the heat, and leave the chicken, covered, to simmer slowly for about three hours. Keep an eye on the water level and make sure the chicken is well covered by adding more liquid if necessary.

Although the traditional soup was served with droplets of fat floating on the top, a version that avoids blocking so many arteries is now more popular. So to get rid of the fat you need to refrigerate the soup. Lift out the chicken and strain the soup into a large bowl, discarding all the cooked vegetables. When it is quite cold the pale layer of fat on the top can easily be removed. (What do you do with the chicken, you may be wondering? It's quite good in sandwiches or a salad.)

To serve the chicken soup, which may have turned to jelly if it is chilled, spoon it back into the pan and bring it to the boil over high heat. Throw in the vermicelli and simmer the soup for about ten minutes, when it will be cooked, and its name will have changed to Lockshen Soup. Make sure you have a steady table and pour it into large bowls.

Casserole of Lamb

Slow–cooked lamb with the meat almost falling off the bones is enjoyed in many different guises. In Ireland it is called Irish Stew, in Lancashire – Hot Pot, Navarin in France and Kleftiko in Greece. The simmering gravy turns into a savoury crust round the edge of the pot. It is so good you can scrape it with a knife and eat the crunchy bits secretly before you take the casserole to the table. You need several large chunks of lamb per person – no nouvelle cuisine portions – because there is a lot of waste.

2¼ lbs	I kg	lamb on the bone (cut into 12 thick slices)
1 – 2 tbsp		oil
2		onions
4		carrots
½ cup		barley
½ cube		beef stock (optional)
few sprigs		fresh rosemary
		boiled potatoes to serve with it

You will need: a large cooking pot that will go on the hob and in the oven (or a non–stick frying pan and an ordinary casserole).
Preheat the oven to 325F, 160C, Gas 3.

Cut the onion into quarters and the carrots into chunks. Place the lamb over the base of the casserole and cook over medium heat until the meat is no longer red, turning it frequently to start cooking all the sides. Pour in the oil, add the quartered onions and continue frying until they start to brown. This will take about five minutes. Sprinkle over the barley, and add the pieces of carrot. Season with plenty of salt and pepper (and half a crumbled beef stock cube if you like a strong gravy) and pour in enough water to cover it all by about an inch (2.5cm). Put the lid on and cook in the oven for about two hours. (Or fry the lamb and onions first in a non–stick pan and transfer them to the casserole with the barley and carrots.) After an hour and a half check to see that the barley has not absorbed all the water and add some more if it has. The meat should have enough liquid to serve as a gravy. If you like rosemary, throw in a large sprig at this stage. When the lamb is tender, carefully pour the gravy into a small pot and leave it to get quite cold (not long if you put it in the freezer). Remove the hard fat and pour the juice back into the casserole.

Reheat gently until the lamb is piping hot, taste for seasoning and serve each portion with a fresh sprig of rosemary and some small boiled potatoes.

Lemon Soufflé

A large soufflé takes over half an hour to cook which leads to the problem of timing it to be ready after the main course. Using individual small pots makes it easier. They can be prepared ahead and take exactly ten minutes to cook — the right amount of time for another glass of wine before dessert. This makes six small ones.

2	lemons (preferably unwaxed ones)
3	eggs (medium size)
4 – 5 tbsp	sugar
	oil or butter for greasing

You will need: 6 small ramekins (3" / 8cm diameter, 5 fl oz / 1 / 4pt capacity) an electric whisk; 2 bowls; a grater or zester; a spatula and a baking tray.

First prepare the ramekins. Grease them and sprinkle a little sugar into each, shaking it to distribute it evenly over the base and sides.

Wash the lemons and grate the rind into one of the bowls. Add the egg yolks and put the whites into the other bowl. Halve the lemons and squeeze the juice into a cup.

Whisk the whites until they begin to lose the transparent frothy look, add one tablespoon of sugar and whisk a little more until they are stiff and white but not very firm. Then whisk the yolks with 3 tablespoons of sugar until they look very pale and thick. This will take a few minutes. Pour in the lemon juice, mixing well and then immediately add a large spoonful of the whites, folding but not beating it in. Add a little more, then with the spatula fold the yolk mixture back into the bowl with the remaining whites, lifting the mixture from the bottom. Take care to use gentle strokes, working quickly to get rid of the blobs of white without letting the mixture deflate. Spoon the uncooked soufflé into the ramekins (they should be almost full) and put them on a baking tray. Put the tray in the coldest part of the fridge where it can stay for about half an hour. *Preheat the oven to 350F, 180C, Gas 4.*

Take the soufflés out of the fridge and leave them at room temperature for up to twenty minutes. Then bake them in the middle of the oven for exactly ten minutes. They will have risen about an inch above the rims and should be brought straight to the table. If you live in a castle and have a long walk from the kitchen to the dining room they will have fallen by the time you get there.

Stuffed Dates in Caramel

It's a good idea to make a small amount of caramel the first time and do it again if you want a large quantity. You start with a sugar syrup. As the water is driven off by fast boiling, the melted sugar begins to burn. At that moment it becomes caramel and has to be dealt with very quickly before it hardens.

1 box		dried dates
For the almond paste:		
2 oz	50g	sugar
3 fl oz	90ml	water
5 oz	150g	ground almonds
		red, green or yellow food colouring
For the caramel:		
4 oz	125g	sugar
6 fl oz	180ml	water
1 dsp		liquid glucose

You will need: a small saucepan; a sugar thermometer (optional); a sheet of foil; some oil; a cocktail stick and paper sweet cases.

For the almond paste filling, put the sugar and water into the pan and bring to the boil. Continue boiling for about two minutes to make a syrup. Pour this on to the ground almonds, mix well and leave to cool. Divide the white paste into three or four pieces and using a cocktail stick, put a couple of dots of colour on to each one. (A tiny drop colours a large amount.) Knead the mixtures until they no longer look marbled. Split about ten dates lengthwise and remove the stones. Fill each one with a small, rolled piece of the coloured paste. Have ready a sheet of foil which has been generously oiled.

For the caramel, put the sugar, water and glucose in a clean pan and cook over low heat to melt the sugar. Stir occasionally until it boils when it should now look like a clear syrup. Continue boiling over medium heat but don't stir it any more. It will bubble and is extremely hot (much hotter than boiling water, so take care). It will then change colour to a pale gold and will gradually turn to a darker brown. Watch it all the time. The colour will tell you when it's ready: about 280F, 140C, if you have a sugar thermometer. You can check by taking a small spoon and pouring a droplet on to the foil. If it sets hard immediately the caramel is ready. Take it off the heat and lower in the dates, one by one. With a fork, turn each date over to make sure it is covered, lift it out and put it on the foil. When the dates are cold, wipe any traces of oil off the bases and stand them in paper cases.

Italian Bean Salad

A suggestion for emergencies – a good idea for the unexpected vegetarian.

I	430g tin	borlotti beans
I	430g tin	cannellini beans
I	285g jar	sun–dried tomatoes in olive oil

You will need: a bowl and a strainer.

Open the tins of beans and pour each one, separately, into the strainer. Rinse with cold water to remove the thick juice. Arrange the beans on a large flat plate in alternate wide strips with a circle of the dried tomatoes round the edge. Drizzle the beans with some oil.

Tagliatelle with Cream and Parmesan

The quickest ever pasta dish for two people, so increase the quantities if you need more.

8 oz	250g	tagliatelle (flat ribbon pasta, curled or long)
¼ pt	150ml	single cream or 5 sticks frozen cream
3 oz	75g	block of parmesan cheese
		salt, black pepper

You will need: a large saucepan; a small saucepan or the microwave; a colander or large strainer and a grater.

Pour enough water into the pan to fill it two thirds full and heat it until it is bubbling. If you are in a hurry boil the water in a kettle first, as it is quicker than boiling large quantities on the hob. Throw in a teaspoon of salt and the tagliatelle and boil for five or six minutes, or until it is just cooked. In a small pan heat the cream gently, but there is no need to have it boiling. Alternatively defrost the cream sticks in a small bowl in the microwave for 4 minutes and heat on **high** for about 45 seconds.

Have ready some heated plates and a large bowl and grate the cheese. Drain the pasta, pour it into the bowl and immediately pour on the warm cream. Grind over plenty of black pepper and sprinkle on some freshly grated parmesan. Toss the pasta to mix in the cream and spoon it on to hot plates. Pass round some extra grated cheese at the table.

Roasted Sea Bass

An expensive fish but one that is trouble free and with large bones that can easily be seen. Serve with boiled new potatoes and french beans.

2 lb	900g	sea bass with the head on
3 – 4 tbsp		olive oil
I		large lemon
some sprigs		mint,chervil,chives (about 4 tbsp when chopped)
		salt, pepper

You will need: a baking tin; a small bowl and a large serving dish.
Preheat the oven to 450F, 230C, Gas 8.

While the oven is heating prepare the fish. Wash it inside and out and dry it well. Put the olive oil in the base of the baking tin and heat it for a few minutes. Put in the fish, turning it over to coat it on both sides. Season with salt and pepper and squeeze over a little lemon juice. Roast it in the hot oven for 15 – 20 minutes. While it is cooking the skin will puff up and brown slightly.

Meanwhile squeeze the rest of the lemon juice into a small bowl. Chop the herbs finely, season with salt and pepper and leave to infuse with the juice while the fish cooks. To see if it is ready, test it with a sharp knife near the bone – if it still looks shiny inside it is not done, if it is white and opaque it is. Pour the roasting oil into the herbed lemon juice and whisk it with a fork. Transfer the fish to a heated dish and serve it with the warm dressing, new potatoes and beans.

Queen of Sheba Cake

I never discovered the origin of the name. Perhaps it might make a triumphant entrance — it is certainly that good.

6 oz	175g	plain dark chocolate
2 tbsp		rum
4 oz	125g	unsalted butter
4 oz	125g	sugar
3		eggs, separated
2 oz	50g	ground almonds
2 oz	50g	plain flour
For the topping:		
2 oz	50g	plain dark chocolate
1 tbsp		rum
2 oz	50g	unsalted butter

You will need: an 8" (20cm) cake tin, with a push-up base, or an ordinary tin with greaseproof paper to line it; three bowls and an electric whisk. Preheat the oven to 350F, 180C, Gas 4.

Grease or line the tin. Melt the chocolate in a bowl. This will take about two minutes on **high** in a microwave oven or can be done over a saucepan of simmering water. Stir in the rum. In another bowl beat the butter and sugar together and then stir in the egg yolks. In a third bowl (sorry, but it is worth it – wait till you eat the cake!) whisk the egg whites until they are stiff. Then beat the melted chocolate into the egg yolk mixture and gently stir in some of the whites. Sprinkle on some of the flour and ground almonds and continue folding in the whites and the rest of the dry ingredients until they are all used up.

Pour the mixture into the tin and bake the cake for about 25 – 30 minutes. The centre should still be moist as this is a cake which is dark and gooey rather than one with a crumb-like texture. Leave it to cool and then make the topping. Melt the remaining chocolate, stir in the rum and beat in the rest of the butter. Put the cake on a large plate, spoon over this glossy sauce and leave in a cold place, but don't put it in the fridge.

The Menu

Roasted Nuts

• • •

Roast Chicken with Chestnut Stuffing

Cranberry Sauce

Potato Latkes

• • •

Chocolate Brownies

_____

Potato Skins with Garlic and Olive Oil

Cream of Tomato Soup

• • •

Mediterranean Salad

• • •

Noodle Pudding

The Techniques

Stuffing and roasting chicken

Making gravy

Shallow frying

Comfort Food

To a Japanese suffering from a hangover, the most appealing food might be a plate of sushi. Raw fish would not be a comforting thought to westerners brought up on shepherd's pie and baked beans on toast. When we are ill or sad, we crave the food of our childhood as if the taste of treats from the past can in some way alleviate the pain of the present.

Of course, if early memories are unhappy, we try to shake them off by moving on to a more discriminating world of food and people. A well-known writer recalled his Kentucky childhood and his grandmother's 'indifferent and bland cooking in a squalid kitchen'. In his mind the food and his religious family were inextricably mingled and brought him no joy. But it is possible to look back on unsophisticated feasts of childhood with affection and still grow up with a discerning palate. One of the brightest stars of British new-wave cuisine is a chef called Alastair Little. He still speaks warmly about his mother's cooking and his North country background.

When I was young, after the war, meat was in short supply and it was never a matter of choosing what to have, but rather accepting the bony fragments that were on offer. The basic rations rarely included chicken but a few farms in Ireland would arrange to dispatch birds to London. There was such excitement in the house when the first parcel arrived. The chilly dining room had to be heated three hours before the meal with a two-bar electric fire. At last the chicken appeared – a crisp roast capon oozing with chestnut stuffing. The taste of that moist, white meat and the crackly skin was my first sensation of luxury.

Although my memories of food at home were happy, like most children, I loathed the food at school. The normal fare at St. Paul's Girls' School was a stew with indeterminate lumps of meat floating in a watery brown gravy. This was followed by dead-man's leg, a two-foot long suet pudding spurting out dark red jam. The Muslims and Jews (like me) who didn't eat meat unless it was halal or kosher, sat at a separate table with the vegetarians, so we had an alternative menu. One of these lunches was a nutritionist's nightmare called 'spaghetti stuffed potatoes' – huge grey jacket potatoes, still hard in the middle with a mound of short-chopped tinned spaghetti running down in a glutinous orange pool.

To compensate for these lunches, I would look forward to the everyday meals we had at home. My father liked unadventurous food and had a passion for bread. In fact he would often sneak into the kitchen after supper and eat a chunk of fresh bread while my brother and I argued over the washing up. Yet bread is the perfect palliative - thin buttered slices for a child who has measles, a creamy bread and butter pudding for an adult with a cold.

The joys of eating are as subjective as personal memories. There is a dining-room in one of the Crown Courts where the judges meet for the lunch break. They discuss the morning's cases over a glass of wine and tuck into steak and kidney pie and apple crumble with thick, tinned custard. They exchange tales about their weekend houses in the country and eat puddings which are reminiscent of the nursery food they ate with nanny. Cut off from the world of diets and health warnings they eat their comforting meal before they go back into court for the afternoon session. No doubt they will meet again in the evening at a sophisticated dinner, but there they will be presented with char-grilled fish and a salad of mixed leaves.

The fashion in food runs in close parallel to the world of clothes. Like long and short skirts, it goes in phases. For decades the diet for a normal day included a cooked breakfast, a substantial lunch and afternoon tea, followed by a four-course dinner. Then came the years of nouvelle cuisine and cuisine minceur. Waiters were choreographed to lift the huge domes in unison, revealing minute quantities of rare meat on a pool of sauce, decorated with three potato balls the size of a cherry. To follow that, comforting meals had to come back. In France it was called Cuisine Grandmère. In England the pudding was revived. It was trendy to serve treacle tart as a dinner party dessert. In hotels and restaurants, no-one was surprised to see sticky toffee pudding on the menu. The supermarkets were quick to cash in on the trend – with skimmed milk at one end of the cold cabinet and cartons of porridge, custard and clotted cream rice pudding at the other.

Modern advertising encourages the link between guilt and food. Cream is naughty. Cake is fattening. Chocolate is wicked. Most of these indulgences take place in private. Women in slim skirts will refuse sugar in their coffee but alone, at home, they will eat far more chocolate than any man. Comfort food is all about eating at home. The recession-hit restaurants would agree with a journalist's observation: "How many people want to go out on a cold winter's night, risking arrest for drunkenness, only to sit fully upright at a table being bright when they would rather be slumped on a sofa at home".

Food can even be a compensation for being away from home. We once spent a weekend in a rented house in Petersfield with some friends called Elkan and Marguerite. The rooms were cold but we stayed up late talking and playing scrabble. We laughed a lot and ate huge meals. On the last evening Marguerite produced an incredible pile of latkes. The small bite-sized version of these potato pancakes are often served at parties. They are so popular that old ladies get pushed aside in the stampede to intercept a plateful before it reaches the buffet table. But Marguerite's latkes were large and sizzling hot, dark on the outside with strands of grated potato and caramelised onion trailing round the edges. They were just as they should be – crisp, brown and too many.

The most comforting, downmarket, unfashionable food of all is a Jewish dish called lockshen pudding. Not for those who are looking for a delicate mouthful, it is thick, filling, and wickedly tasty. You eat it while you are wearing old clothes and relaxing. (No one will admit to liking this so it will rarely be served after a normal meal.) Don't worry that it is bad for you. You can make up for it by exercising – starting with a brisk walk into the kitchen for just another slice.

Apart from the roast chicken, the recipes in this chapter are filling and fast. The whole point of comfort food is that when you feel like eating it, you don't want to wait. Everything in the second menu is just enough for one or two. It would make a perfect TV dinner - not the tray of reheated frozen food that this term normally conjures up, but a treat, to be eaten on one's lap, alone, in front of a television programme that no-one else will tolerate.

Roasted Nuts

Of course you can buy a packet of nuts in any local shop. By the time you've found some money and walked round the corner you could be taking these out of the oven.

12 oz	350g	raw mixed nuts, (cashews, peanuts, almonds)
2 -3 tbsp		oil
For sweet nuts:		
I tbsp		sugar
¼ tsp		cinnamon
For savoury nuts:		
I tsp		salt

You will need: a large baking sheet and 2 plates.
Preheat the oven to 350F, 180C, Gas 4.

When the oven is nearly hot, spoon the oil on to the tin and put it inside to heat slightly. After a minute or two take it out and throw all the nuts on to the tin, shaking it well so that they are lightly coated. Roast the nuts for about 10 minutes when they should be crisp and brown.

While they are cooking get ready two plates. On one put the salt and on the other put a mixture of sugar and cinnamon. Take out the nuts and shake half on to each plate. Spoon over the seasoning and leave them to cool. Pour the roasted nuts into separate bowls and try not to eat them all at once.

Potato Latkes

Latkes can be a meal on their own, served with sour cream and apple sauce or even the gooseberry purée on page 52. Here, they are fried (preferably by somebody else) just before you serve the main course.

12 oz	350g	medium sized potatoes (about 4)
1		onion
1½		eggs
2 tbsp		medium matzo meal (optional)
lots of		salt and pepper
		oil for frying

You will need: a grater or food processor with a grating disc; a colander or sieve; a large frying pan and some paper towels.

Grate the potatoes and the onion into a colander or large sieve. Press them down and squeeze out the thick starchy liquid which comes out. In a bowl beat the eggs and then stir in the drained potatoes and the onions. If you have the matzo meal, which you can buy at a Jewish deli, put it in as well. It is coarsely ground unleavened bread which adds a bit of flavour and crunch. Add plenty of seasoning.

Pour in enough oil to cover the base of the frying pan and heat it for about a minute. Place spoonfuls of the mixture all over the pan. The oil should sizzle as soon as the first pancake goes in, but make sure they are not too close together as the latkes will spread. Flatten them with the spoon so they are about half an inch (1.2cm) thick and fry until the underside is crisp and brown. Turn them over and brown the other side. Drain the latkes on paper towels and serve immediately.

Roast Chicken with Chestnut Stuffing

Stuffing the chicken under the skin helps to keep the breast succulent so it is marvellous cold, too. The contrast of white meat and dark stuffing looks good on a large platter.

5 lb	2kg	fresh (not frozen) free range roasting chicken
		giblets (often packed inside the chicken)
2		onions (keep 1 for the stuffing)
1		carrot
7 oz	200g	unsweetened chestnut purée (about half a tin)
2½ oz	70g	fresh breadcrumbs (about a cupful)
2 - 3 tbsp		oil
		salt, pepper

You will need: a blender or processor to make the breadcrumbs; a needle and cotton (optional); a roasting tin and a small piece of foil; a small saucepan; a small frying pan; a small bowl and an electric carving knife if you are serving the chicken cold.

Put the giblets into a small pan with a peeled onion and carrot. Cover with cold water and bring it to the boil. Turn down the heat and simmer the stock while the chicken is cooking. It will be used for the gravy. (Don't worry if you have no giblets, water will do instead of this stock.)

Wash the chicken, inside and out, and dry it very well with paper towels. Put your hand under the skin at the back and easing forwards, lift the skin away from the breast, taking care not to break it. This is where the stuffing is going – not in the cavity of the carcase.

Chop the onion finely and sauté it, in a few tablespoons of hot oil, in the frying pan. When it is beginning to brown, lower the heat, pour on half a cup of boiling water and then turn it off and leave the onion to absorb some of the liquid. Mak e the breadcrumbs by taking some thick slices of bread and blending or processing them until they form crumbs. Mix together the onion, the crumbs and the chestnut purée, adding salt and pepper to season the mixture. Leave the stuffing to cool completely before filling the chicken.

Preheat the oven to 425F, 220C, Gas 7.

Press the stuffing underneath the skin all over the breast. Any gaps in the skin at each end can be sewn up with needle and cotton: this couture touch stops the stuffing oozing out during the cooking, but isn't vital. Brush the tin with a little oil and put the chicken in, breast side down. Prick the skin of the legs to release the fat. Roast the chicken for half an hour. Take it out and holding it carefully, pour off any fat and juices into a small bowl. Put the chicken back in the oven, turning it over so that the breast side is uppermost. Continue cooking at *400F, 200C, Gas 6* for another 45 minutes, occasionally pouring off the fat. If the top is looking very brown, cover the breast with a small piece of foil. To see if the chicken is done, press the tip of a sharp knife into one of the legs. If the juices run clear it is cooked – otherwise leave it until the flesh is no longer pink. (It is very important to make sure that chicken is well cooked. The legs always take longer than the breast and this method of stuffing the bird helps to keep the white meat moist while the legs become tender.) Lift the chicken on to a serving dish and keep it warm while you make the gravy.

Pour away the fat and add the juices to the roasting tin with about a cup of stock or water. Put the tin on the hob and heat the gravy, stirring in any brown crispy bits, and boil it for a few minutes. This deglazing of the pan makes a concentrated chicken-flavoured sauce without using cubes. Carve the chicken and serve the gravy separately in a small jug.

Cranberry Sauce

Cranberries are the official accompaniment to roast turkey at Thanksgiving but this sauce is brilliant with chicken.

12 oz	350g	cranberries
6 oz	175g	sugar
9 fl oz	250ml	water
1		orange
2 dsp		Grand Marnier
		nutmeg

You will need: a saucepan; a bowl; a strainer and a grater.

Wash the cranberries. Put the sugar and water in the pan and heat slowly until the sugar has dissolved. Bring the syrup to the boil, add the cranberries and continue boiling for about ten minutes. Stir in the grated zest and juice of the orange. Add the Grand Marnier, grate over a little nutmeg and leave the sauce to cool.

Chocolate Brownies

American brownies are a cross between cookies, which are biscuits, and a cake.
The mixture can be made by a child (or an adult without an electric mixer) and
the finished squares are rich and chewy.

5 oz	140g	plain chocolate
4 oz	112g	unsalted butter
4 oz	112g	self raising flour
4 oz	112g	sugar
2		eggs
1 tsp		vanilla essence
3 oz	85g	halved pecan nuts

You will need: a medium sized bowl, big enough to mix all the ingredients;
a microwave or a small saucepan; a baking tin about 10" (25cm) square and
greaseproof paper.
Preheat the oven to 400F, 200C, Gas 6.

Rub the paper from the butter over the greaseproof paper and press
it on to the baking tin (if your tin is non-stick, you won't need to use
paper). Put the chocolate and the butter into the bowl and microwave
on **medium** for about two minutes or until the chocolate has melted.
Alternatively, do this over a pan of simmering water. Break the eggs
into a cup and beat them together briefly. Mix the flour, sugar and the
eggs into the chocolate mixture and beat well until the brownie
mixture is smooth. Pour it into the baking tin. It's important not to
use a tin that is too large, otherwise the mixture will spread out and
be too thin. If yours is too big, fold a sheet of foil into a strip about an
inch (2.5cm) deep and use it to cover one end of the tin. Arrange the
halved pecans in rows and bake the chocolate brownies for 20
minutes. By this time the mixture will be just set and slightly firmer
at the edges. Leave it to cool and then cut it into squares.

Potato Skins with Garlic and Olive Oil

3	large potatoes (skins only)
2 - 3 tbsp	olive oil
I clove	garlic
	sea salt

You will need: a large baking tin.
Preheat the oven to 375F, 190C, Gas 5.

Wash the potatoes well. With a sharp knife cut off the potato peel very thickly and keep the potatoes, covered with cold water, for another use. Precook the skins briefly, either in an uncovered pan in the microwave on **high** for 2 minutes, or in boiling water in a saucepan for the same time. (If you boil them you have to drain them well.) Pour the oil on to the tin, cut the garlic clove in half, and holding one half in each hand, rub it all over the tin to spread and flavour the oil. Dip one side of the skins in the oil and turn them over, arranging them in a single layer. Cook for about 25 minutes, turning them again after 15 to brown both sides. Lift the crisp potato skins on to some kitchen paper and eat them hot or warm.

Cream of Tomato Soup

The essence of a quick treat is that you don't need to go out and buy anything. In case there's no cream in the fridge, frozen cream sticks are a good stand-by. They are great for moments like this where a small amount is wanted.

2 fl oz	50ml	fresh single cream or 2 frozen sticks
½ pt	300ml	tomato juice
I tsp		tomato purée
		salt, black pepper
I dsp		Harvey's Bristol Cream Sherry

You will need: a 1pt (570ml) jug or bowl or a small saucepan.

For frozen cream, microwave it on **defrost** for one minute or leave it out until it softens (this takes much longer).

Mix the tomato juice with the purée and seasoning and heat gently until it boils. You can do this in the microwave on **high** for 3 minutes, or in a saucepan over low heat. Have ready a large soup bowl and pour in the tomato mixture. Immediately stir in the sweet sherry and then spoon in the cream, swirling it around. Eat it straight away.

Mediterranean Salad

A collection of cold cooked vegetables can be quickly turned into a large bowl of salad. All you need to add is some pasta or potatoes, or pile on anything else you fancy. Tuna would make it like Salade Niçoise, or cold meat would turn it into what is called a Chef's Salad in hotel room service menus.

½ lb	225g	small new potatoes (preferably Jersey) or
6 oz	150g	pasta (fusilli or farfalle)
3 oz	75g	french beans
1		courgette
1		small cos lettuce or 2 little gem lettuces
1		small red pepper
1		small yellow pepper
5		black olives
6		radishes
1 tbsp		olive oil
For the vinaigrette:		
3 tbsp		red wine vinegar
½ tsp		mustard
		salt, pepper
6-8 tbsp		olive oil

You will need: a large saucepan; a small covered pot for the microwave or a small frying pan and a small saucepan.

Boil the new potatoes in enough salted water to cover them and cook for about 12 minutes or until they are tender when tested with a sharp knife. If you are using pasta, boil it in the usual way in plenty of salted water and drain it after about ten minutes. Cook the french beans in water on the hob or in the microwave (about 2 minutes on **high** with 2 tablespoons of water). Cut the courgette into sticks and sauté in oil in a small pan (or in the microwave, uncovered, for 4 minutes on **high**). Drain the potatoes and beans and leave all the vegetables to cool slightly.

Arrange wedges of lettuce around the edge of a large bowl. Cut the peppers into rings (discarding the inner membrane) and lay them on top. Mix the cooked pasta or potatoes with the beans and the courgette and pile it all into the centre. Scatter over the olives and radishes.

Mix together the vinaigrette ingredients and just before you are ready to eat, pour it over the salad and toss it well.

Noodle Pudding

The official name is lockshen pudding, meaning noodles or vermicelli. It's another good way to use up cooked pasta and should be served warm - neither mouthburningly hot nor fridge cold. The quantity for one is best done in the microwave. For more people - and double the amount - it's worth lighting the oven.

2 oz	50g	vermicelli or 4 oz/100g cooked noodles
¼ pt	150ml	milk
1		egg
1 tbsp		raisins or sultanas
1 tbsp		vanilla sugar (see page 81)
1 tsp		butter (optional)

You will need: a large saucepan; a bowl; an ovenproof dish (about 2pt/1 litre capacity) or a shallow glass microwave dish.
Preheat the oven to 350F, 180C, Gas 4.

Cook the noodles in boiling water (or use previously boiled ones). Drain but don't rinse them. Mix the milk with the egg, raisins and sugar in a bowl. To cook in the microwave, arrange the noodles in the glass dish, pour over the milk mixture and cook on **medium** power for 6 minutes, stirring once or twice as the outside tends to cook quicker than the centre. When you take it out, the custard should be just set. It continues to harden a bit as it cools and is nice if parts of it are still creamy.

To make a larger quantity, rub the butter all round the inside of the ovenproof dish. Whisk together the eggs, sugar, milk and raisins. Put the cooked noodles into the buttered dish, pour over the egg mixture and stir until they are well coated. Bake for about 30 minutes until the custard is just set.

The Menus

Globe Artichokes with Lemon Sauce

Rice Pudding

Cucumber Trunks with Dill and Fish Salad

Coffee Sponge Pudding

Semolina Gnocchi with Red Pesto

Bread and Butter Pudding

Smoked Haddock and Spinach

French Apple Flan

The Techniques

Using the combination microwave

Microwaving sauces and puddings

Combinations

Imagine going to a garden centre to choose a lawnmower. There are some which will tackle three square feet of turf and others which are designed to roam effortlessly through the grounds of Blenheim Palace. Basically they both do the same job of cutting the grass. Microwaves also come in two versions: economy and luxury. But the difference is not in size. The more complicated ones have timers, built-in heat sensors and autocook facilities. These are useful if you want the machine to calculate when your frozen chicken tikka will be ready while you have a shower. What you need if you want to cook with a microwave is a turntable, an accurate timer, understanding and practice.

In the preceding chapters I've suggested using the microwave for softening ingredients (potatoes, aubergines, chocolate), for sauces (berries, tomatoes) and occasionally for desserts. It works best with small quantities since the more you cook the longer it takes. If you have to double up on cooking times it's not the best way to do the job. If you have been using the instructions for the microwave rather than the longer method, you'll probably find that your cooking is getting better and you're spending far less time in the kitchen.

The title 'Combinations' refers to using microwave power in combination with conventional power. Microwaves alone are good for vegetables, fish and fruit, and ghastly for meat, cakes and pastries. A combination oven gives you the facility to bake or grill, while the food gets a simultaneous low blast of microwave heat. This cuts down on the time, so that jacket potatoes, cakes and puddings will brown on top and cook quicker inside.

However, a far more helpful combination is to use the moist heat and low power to whip up a sauce or steam a pudding while the dry heat of your oven is coping with the main course. Instead of spending a tedious half hour stirring egg yolks or semolina or waiting twice that time for a couple of artichokes and a creamy pudding to be ready, you can have the whole meal on the table quickly and spend more time relaxing afterwards.

The organisation of a meal isn't just a matter of making dishes in isolation. As you get more experienced you'll get better at assessing which recipes are going to be time-consuming and what you can be doing while you wait for something to cook.

On the next page are some ideas of what you can do in less than a minute.

- Cut a large firm lemon in two. With the cut side down on a plate, microwave one half for 20 seconds on **high**. It will yield one more tablespoon of juice than the other half.

- 50 seconds on **defrost** will bring a 5 oz/150g piece of refrigerated brie back to the just ripe delicatessen state. It is better not to use a pointed wedge as the tip might go runny.

- A few dried apricots in a cup, covered in water or Grand Marnier, plump up with a brief burst of **high** power. Sultanas can absorb strained tea in a similar way. Restoring dried fruit to its original size used to take about an hour and can now be done in a minute.

- Peel and crush a couple of cloves of garlic. Drop them into half a cup of olive oil and cook on **high** for 30 seconds. They will release a powerful aroma. Black olives will work too, and both the flavoured oils can be used to drizzle over cooked vegetables or in frying. (If, instead, you put the garlic in the pan with the oil, it can easily burn.)

- A cold scone or a slice of fruit cake will taste fresher after a 10 second burst on **high** . The fat in cakes often makes them heavy when they are cold and this helps to bring back the just-baked taste.

- Nuts are one of the few foods which brown in the microwave. The usual way to make toasted almonds or hazelnuts is under the grill where they get partially burnt or in a preheated oven, where they get totally burnt if you forget them. Spread 1oz (25g) flaked almonds on some kitchen paper. After a minute on **high** they will start to brown and 30 seconds later they should be crisp and golden. You can do hazelnuts the same way – the time depends on the quantity.

A few moments spent doing any of these will be far more fun than struggling to decipher complicated instructions. It is all there in the combination oven manual but what on earth do you key in to auto-preheat-delay-start a frozen beefburger? Working my way through a book of recipes for kippers in marmalade sauce and sprout and stilton soup, I never did discover how to adapt the pre-set programmes to anything I wanted to make. There is no explanation of the seemingly random combinations of hot dry heat and low microwave power. In fact, it's much harder to judge the moment when the centre of a cook-chill shepherd's pie is hot, than to try out far more sophisticated dishes from scratch. Apart from this, there is one other disadvantage. The grill or baking tray of a multi-purpose cooker gets very hot. After you've cooked a leg of lamb, you can't then microwave a plate of vegetables. With a simple microwave oven the inside doesn't get hot and it turns itself off. This makes it safer to use and is a tremendous benefit for children or anyone who is forgetful. For people with poor sight or frail fingers it's invaluable.

To dwell on the downside of a cooker like this would be mean. If you have a very small kitchen and don't have room for a separate oven and microwave, it could be a good investment. It will bake and grill and you'll enjoy the benefits of three methods of cooking in one box.

The manuals that come with these machines are, of course, not that hard to decipher and they have some helpful hints on defrosting and how to arrange food. However, they often mention a term called 'standing time'. This generally refers to meat and dense cakes, meaning that the cooking continues after the food has been taken out of the oven, so this has to be included in the time calculation. Since I don't recommend using the microwave for these foods I would suggest, on the contrary, that you should eat a dish as soon as it is cooked. Briefly poached fish loses heat quickly and the colour of vegetables deteriorates if they are left standing in liquid.

There are four menus in this chapter but none of them includes a main course. The gap can be filled with any of the roasts or grills you've already mastered. By concentrating on starters and puddings you'll see how easy it is to make two dishes in the time it would have taken you to prepare one. The first few recipes are for two people; using the microwave at its best where it would hardly be worth heating the oven for an hour when eight minutes will produce the same result. Don't be tempted to double the quantities because that will affect the timing. The later recipes all serve four, as usual. They are almost as quick as going out for a take-away and a lot more exciting.

Globe Artichokes with Lemon Sauce

Artichokes are one of the most leisurely of starters, eaten slowly and never hurried. Yet the preparation can be speeded up considerably. The sauce is similar to a hollandaise, but that uses butter and has to be served hot. This oil-based one is better cold.

2		large artichokes
4 tbsp		boiling water
		salt, pepper
I		lemon (using half for the sauce)
For the sauce:		
2		egg yolks
I tsp		wine or cider vinegar
		salt, pepper
4 fl oz	125ml	olive oil

You will need: a glass or china dish large enough to hold both artichokes; microwaveable cling film; a large bowl and a small bowl; a whisk or a fork; a small jug (not metal) and the microwave.

First prepare the artichokes. Cut off the stems close to the base with a sharp knife. Unless the artichokes are extremely fresh and have no brown bits, cut across the top of the leaves and take off the points of the lower, outer leaves. Immediately wash the artichokes, rub the cut edge with the lemon and drop them into a large bowl of cold water. Squeeze the lemon and add half the juice to the water. (This helps to keeps the colour bright and is called 'acidulated water'.)

Arrange the artichokes side by side with the stem down, on the cooking dish. Add a little salt to the boiling water and sprinkle it on top. Wrap round a large piece of film and make two small slits in the top to release the steam. Cook on **high** for 6 minutes. Carefully lift off the film, opening it on the side furthest away from you to avoid getting burnt from the rush of steam. Turn the artichokes over and cook for a further 4 minutes, using a fresh piece of film if it can't be re-used. To test if they are done, press a knife into the base and see if it is soft. Leave to cool slightly and then open out the top leaves. Remove the hairy choke with a spoon, being careful not to damage the heart while you do this. Arrange the artichokes on individual plates.

For the sauce: Whisk the egg yolks with a tablespoon of lemon juice and the wine vinegar in the small bowl. Season lightly with salt and pepper. Heat the oil, in the jug, on **high** for 30 seconds and then start pouring it in a thin stream on to the egg yolks. As you pour it with one hand, whisk it constantly with the other, slowly adding the oil until it thickens slightly. This is called an emulsion and is basically what happens when you make mayonnaise. It's tiring on the wrist, but don't be tempted to throw in all the oil, as you have to make sure each bit is absorbed before you continue pouring.

Put the bowl in the microwave and cook on **defrost** for just over a minute, taking it out to stir two or three times. It should now look thick. Pour in the other tablespoon of lemon juice and whisk it once more. Now, if it happens that you overcook it slightly, it may curdle, that is, it will separate and you will see immediately that it doesn't look smooth. Don't worry. Get an ice cube and quickly stir it in, whisking fast until it has melted. By this time the sauce will almost certainly be thick and smooth again. Leave it to cool and serve it with the artichokes, pouring some into the centre and passing round the rest separately.

Rice Pudding with Vanilla

Old–fashioned rice pudding takes about two hours to cook and has an almost mushy consistency. The microwave version takes a quarter of the time and leaves the grains slightly crunchy. It's a matter of taste but I think it's better to remove the skin and serve the rice cold.

½ cup	pudding rice
2 cups	boiling water
2 cups	milk
2 tbsp	vanilla sugar with the pod (see page 81)

You will need: a large deep glass or china bowl (4 pt / 2.25l capacity); a strainer and the microwave.

Put the rice in the strainer, rinse it in cold water and put it in the bowl. Pour on the boiling water and microwave uncovered on **high** for 3 minutes. Drain off the water and cover the rice with the milk and add the vanilla sugar with a piece of pod. Cook on **high** for 13 minutes, stirring once about half way through. The milk will rise considerably (that's why you need such a large bowl) and then sink again. After this time the pudding will be cooked, but the rice will still have a 'bite'. With a spoon take off the skin from the top and discard it. Stir the rice again and leave it to cool, when it will absorb some of the milk. This amount fills a couple of cereal bowls – enough for two, or if you're very hungry, one for now and the other for a little later.

Cucumber Trunks with Dill and Fish Salad

Chunks of cucumber can sometimes be watery, so microwaving them briefly gets rid of the moisture but keeps the crunch and colour. Don't put the filling in too early, otherwise they will go soggy.

I		cucumber
I		spring onion
		small bunch of fresh dill
I fl oz	25ml	milk
8 oz	225g	fresh cod fillet, skinned
3 oz	75g	shelled broad beans (about 12 oz/350g in pods)
2 tbsp		mayonnaise
I tbsp		thick cream or crème fraîche
		salt, pepper

You will need: a bowl; a shallow dish with a cover; kitchen paper; a strainer and the microwave.

Chop the spring onion and put it, with a few sprigs of dill, milk and seasoning into the bowl. Cook on **high** for 30 seconds and leave it to infuse while it cools.

With a fork make some thin lines along the cucumbers and cut them into two inch (5cm) lengths. Scoop out the centre seeds with a sharp knife. Stand these trunks on absorbent paper, sprinkle with salt and leave to drain off some of their liquid for about 20 minutes.

Cut the fish into chunks and arrange them in the shallow dish. Strain over the milk, cover and cook on **high** for about a minute. The fish should be just cooked, so that you can flake it easily with a fork. Leave it to cool and then strain off the liquid.

Cook the beans with 2 tablespoons of lightly salted water on **high** for about 3 minutes. Push them out of the tough skins and leave to cool. Dry the cucumber chunks and put a sheet of paper in the microwave. Stand the cucumber chunks evenly around the paper and cook on **high**, uncovered, for a minute. Take them out and leave to cool between fresh sheets of paper to absorb the moisture.

Mix the flaked fish with the cooked beans, mayonnaise and cream and season well. Spoon the filling into the cucumber trunks and stand them upright on a serving dish with some sprigs of fresh dill over the top.

Coffee Sponge Pudding

No-one would contemplate making individual puddings like this if it involved the normal method of steaming for an hour or two. This recipe is fun. You can't get it ready in advance, but the five minute preparation and one minute cooking time is quite theatrical, so invite a friend to watch it happen.

For the sauce:

2 sticks		frozen whipping cream (3 – 4 tbsp fresh cream)
I tbsp		golden syrup
For the pudding:		
I oz	25g	butter
8		pecan nuts
½ tsp		instant coffee granules
I tbsp		brown sugar
I		large egg
I oz	25g	self raising flour

You will need: a small bowl; a slightly larger bowl; 2 cups or ramekins (6 floz / 175ml capacity) with no metal or gold tr im; a small jug or bowl; a strainer and the microwave.

First make the sauce. In the small bowl, defrost the cream sticks on the lowest setting for 1 minute. Melt the golden syrup on a saucer on **high** for 20 seconds. Pour half of it into the cream and mix well.

In the larger bowl melt the butter for 20 seconds on **high**. Arrange four pecans on the base of each cup and pour over a teaspoonful of the butter. Swirl it round and pour in the rest of the golden syrup. Pour a tablespoon of boiling water over the coffee granules and mix them up till they dissolve. Now everything is ready to assemble the puddings. Stir the sugar into the butter, throw in the egg, beating well and then sift the flour into the bowl through the strainer. Pour in the coffee and mix the batter quickly to make it smooth, then spoon it into the two cups on top of the pecans.

Put the cups in the microwave, well apart, and cook on **high** for one minute. Something amazing will happen. The puddings will rise to almost an inch above the rims, then subside slightly. They will look very soft but you should take them out, run a knife around each one and turn it out on to a plate, arranging the nuts on the top, if they have got displaced. Stir the cream sauce and pour it round the puddings. Eat them straight away because they are not good cold, though it's hardly surprising that they don't retain heat like a pudding that has been steamed for two hours.

Semolina Gnocchi with Red Pesto

Gnocchi are dumplings, made of either potato or semolina. The authentic Roman version contains saffron and takes a long time to cook before the mixture can be formed into rounds. The microwave drastically reduces this stage but they still need to be chilled for at least an hour before they are baked. The uncooked sauce goes well with these less perfumed gnocchi. The idea comes from my inventive son in the USA so for once I use cup measurements which are far more sensible than our method of weighing dry things and squinting at jug markings for liquids.

8 oz	225g	semolina
1¼ pts	725ml	milk
		salt, pepper
6 oz	175g	block parmesan cheese (some for sauce below)
1		egg yolk
1 oz	25g	butter
For the pesto sauce:		
1 cup		basil
1 cup		pine nuts
1 cup		sun–dried tomatoes in olive oil
1 cup		grated parmesan cheese (from amount above)
2 cloves		garlic
1 cup		olive oil
½ tsp		salt

You will need: a large glass or china bowl; a cheese grater (because ready grated parmesan in cylindrical pots tastes like sawdust); a shallow tin; a sheet of greaseproof paper or foil; a round biscuit cutter about two and a half inch (5cm) diameter; a large ovenproof dish; a food processor and the microwave.

Put the semolina, milk and a little salt in the bowl. Microwave on **high** for about six minutes, stirring a couple of times till it is very thick. Grate all the cheese and stir 1oz (25g) of it into the semolina with the butter and the egg yolk, beating well till the mixture is smooth. Line the tin with paper or foil and spread the mixture out evenly so that it is about half an inch (1.5cm) deep. Cover and leave it to get quite cold and then cut it into rounds or squares, if you have no cutter.

Preheat the oven to 425F, 220C, Gas 7

Butter the ovenproof dish well, particularly round the top rim, and arrange the round gnocchi in a single layer, overlapping a few if there are too many to fit. Sprinkle over 2oz (50g) of parmesan and some pepper and dot over the remaining butter. Bake for about 30 minutes when the top will be crisp and golden brown.

For the red pesto sauce, put half the pine nuts in the food processor and using the pulse button, buzz them up until they are chopped. Don't let them get like ground almonds as this is too fine. Set them aside, with the rest of the grated cheese. Then blend together the basil, the dried tomatoes, the garlic and a cupful of oil (using some of the flavoured oil from the jar if you like). Throw in the rest of the pine nuts and grind for a few more seconds. Stir in the cheese and nuts you have already chopped. The cool pesto should be spooned over each portion of hot crispy gnocchi.

Bread and Butter Pudding

The fashionable restaurant version of this old favourite uses a mixture of cream and milk and the top is brushed with apricot jam. This is less sweet and rich and is a triumph for the combination oven, achieving a slow-cooked pudding with a crisp top in fifteen minutes.

6		thin slices of bread without crusts
I oz	25g	butter
2 tbsp		sultanas
I tbsp		sherry, brandy or wine
15 fl oz	450ml	milk
2		eggs
2 – 3 tbsp		sugar

You will need: a glass or china dish (a round one measuring 10" or 25cm diameter or an oblong one measuring 8"× 10", 20×25cm); a jug; a strainer; a combination oven (or a normal oven).

Butter the bread and use the butter paper to grease the sides and base of the dish. Cut the bread into triangles and put them in, overlapping slightly. Put the sultanas on a saucer, cover with the sherry and microwave on **high** for 30 seconds to plump them up. Sprinkle them over the bread slices.

With a fork mix the eggs with the milk and sugar, whisking to break up the yolks. Strain this custard over the buttered bread so that there are no lumps of egg. Leave the pudding to stand for about 15 minutes so that the custard is partly absorbed by the bread. Cook it for 15 minutes on combination 250C 160W.

If you don't have a combination oven, preheat a normal oven to 350F, 180C, Gas 4 and cook the pudding for about an hour.

Smoked Haddock and Spinach

The pastry wrapping of fish 'en croûte' is heavy for a starter. This is much lighter and the dark green spinach contrasts well with the pale yellow fish. For taste, the even paler, uncoloured smoked haddock is better but like all natural foods, it is more expensive. Both, however, are quite salty.

12 oz	330g	filleted smoked haddock
2 oz	50g	unsalted butter
1 tsp		whole grain mustard
4 tsp		chopped parsley or dill
1 lb	450g	fresh spinach (8 large leaves)
		pepper (no salt)

You will need: a dish with a lid; a shallow glass or china dish large enough to take the fish in one layer; a cocktail stick; the microwave and paper towels.

Cut the fish into eight pieces and pour over some boiling water. After five minutes drain it well. This is to remove some of the salty taste. Dry the fish with paper towels. Put the butter on a plate and mash in the mustard and chopped herbs.

Wash the spinach very well, remove the stalks and microwave the leaves on **high** with no extra water for half a minute, or until they are just wilted but not cooked. Arrange the spinach on a long sheet of paper towels and cover with some more, pressing down lightly to absorb any moisture. Lay the smoked haddock on the dried leaves. Divide the butter into eight and spread a little on to each piece of fish and then enclose it completely in the spinach. Arrange the parcels in a flat dish, with the join underneath. With a cocktail stick, prick a few holes through the spinach in several places, cover and microwave on **high** for about 3 minutes. Test one parcel by turning it over and lifting off the spinach to see if the fish will flake. If so, it is cooked, otherwise continue for another minute. The butter will ooze out and you can spoon a little over the fish before serving.

French Apple Flan

A guest once asked me which pâtisserie I used and couldn't believe that this dessert came from my own kitchen. In fact, I'd quickly assembled a frozen flan case and the brilliantly quick filling. In France, the traditional way is to bake everything slowly together.

I lb	450g	pastry (see page 36)
3		eating apples
2		large cooking apples
2 tbsp		sugar
4 tbsp		apricot jam

You will need: a flan tin (about 10" / 25cm diameter) with a removable base; a palette knife; some foil; a sieve and the microwave.
Preheat the oven to 425F, 220C, Gas 7.

Roll out the pastry and cut a circle which is at least two inches (5cm) larger than the flan tin. Ease the palette knife underneath to make sure the pastry is not sticking. Lift the pastry carefully into the flan tin, pressing it into the base, but not stretching it. With a fork flatten the pastry all round the side of the tin, leaving any overlap to fall outside. Then take the rolling pin and roll it across the top, pressing down lightly to cut off the spare strip.

To stop the pastry rising or caving in, you should bake it 'blind'. This means weighing it down for the first ten minutes of cooking time and can be done either by lining it with a sheet of foil, pressed into the edges, or with a sheet of greaseproof paper, weighed down with some dried beans. Then remove the foil or paper and leave the pastry cooking for another ten minutes. Take it out of the oven and leave it to cool.

Peel and core the cooking apples and cut them into small pieces. Sprinkle with the sugar and microwave, covered, on **high** for about 4 minutes or until they are soft enough to mash with a fork. Leave them to cool on a plate. Peel the eating apples and cut them into thin slices. Arrange them on a flat plate and microwave, uncovered, on **high** for about 2 minutes. They will be just soft but should not lose their shape. Heat the jam for half to one minute on **high** on a saucer.

To assemble the flan: spoon the cool stewed apple into the flan case. Arrange the slices in circles round the top. Strain the jam through a small sieve and brush it over the apples, making sure the slices are well covered. Carefully press up the removable base and slide the dessert on to a flat plate.

The Menu

Jerusalem Artichoke Soup

• • •

Lamb, Lentils and Apricots

Boiled or Fried Rice

Cabbage Leaves Stuffed with Chestnut

Corn on the Cob

Spinach Parcels with Peas

• • •

Carrot (or Passion) Cake

Strawberries with Orange Juice

The Techniques

Nothing new – you've nearly learned them all

Surprises

It's surprising what you can learn from reading cookery books. At a shop in London called "Booksfor Cooks" ther e are over eight thousand titles. Each one is filled with information. For example: "A single egg white (clearly labelled) can be frozen in an ice cube container, and stored for up to six months. It is best allowed to thaw in the refrigerator." When I read this I was perplexed. Surely everyone can always find or borrow half an egg and if you need one that urgently you wouldn't want to wait for the slow defrosting process.

Newspaper articles sometimes feature prize-winning recipes. A mystery to me was one for porridge. The instructions suggested soaking the oats overnight and finishing off the dish by simmering it for an hour in the morning. Who wants to get up and wait that long for a dish that can take five minutes? All you do to transform the original recipe is put half a cup of porridge oats in a very large bowl with a cup and a half of milk. Microwave it on full power for four minutes, stirring it halfway through. While you look for the brown sugar it will cool slightly to a creamy consistency.

Unlike the wonderful microwaved porridge, food can sometimes be a nasty surprise. The Duke of Edinburgh was obviously thoroughly fed up with official banquets when he said :"I never see any home cooking. All I get is fancy stuff." Nora Ephron, the food writer and film director, claims that nobody really likes capers. "The truth is," she says, " that any dish that tastes good with capers in it, tastes even better with capers not in it."

It's a wonder that certain foods ever got to the table at all. Whoever persevered beyond all that hairy stuff to discover that artichokes are worth eating? Who worked out that the bland avocado would never ripen on the tree and needed to be picked first, and then thought of adding the essential seasoning and vinaigrette? Compared to an ordinary pear, the first taste must have seemed little better than a pot of green face cream.

Once you are interested in cooking, you'll discover many amazing things. Chickens aren't born with their giblets packed inside in plastic bags; liver gets tougher the longer you cook it. Frozen strawberries defrost in a mush but blueberries stay firm. A pound of raw spinach fills a shopping bag but hardly covers a saucer when cooked. Meat cooked on a gas-fired barbecue is just as good as if it were grilled over charcoal; butter beans don't taste of butter. You can read about all these things if you browse through enough books. But did you also know about low-fat crisps being more more fattening than ordinary ones? That's because they come in larger packs and since it's impossible to leave a half empty pack of crisps, you end up eating more.

The menu for this chapter is full of the unexpected. It includes a soup that's hard to identify and three vegetables with surprise wrappings. Unless you believe in old-fashioned steaming, the only way to cook these is in the microwave. But first, here's an alphabetical list of curious bits of information.

Asparagus

White asparagus which is grown without light, is much prized in France. The green 'grass' as it is called after the trade name 'sparrowgrass', doesn't have such tough stems so there is more to eat. There is a good reason why napkins and fingerbowls were always provided – wet asparagus drips down your arm and soaks your sleeves.

Bagels

According to legend a baker in Poland devised some stirrup-shaped rolls to commemorate a battle victory. These were later called bagels (or beigels). Far more interesting is the strange fact that they have to be boiled before they are baked. As they rise to the top of the boiling water, the density of the dough is altered and much of the starch is removed.

Chillies

These tiny peppers can burn your nose and throat, but even before you eat them, the trouble starts. They can irritate the skin and cause agony if you rub your eyes while you're dealing with them. Plastic gloves are the answer.

Doughnuts

When President John F. Kennedy made his famous comment: "Ich bin ein Berliner", he was actually saying "I am a doughnut". He should have left out the indefinite article and said "Ich bin Berliner".

Eggs

Manufacturers have come up with two original ideas – one is the square egg and the other is the Danish long egg. The first comes out of a gadget that presses a warm hard-boiled egg into a specially shaped container, so that the result looks like a cube. The second is a boon for caterers who want to use frozen egg slices. Yolks and whites are poured separately into a cylinder and when cooked the resulting long egg makes forty slices.

Frozen Grapes

You can freeze seedless grapes for a few hours (not days because they will spoil). Arrange them on a pool of strawberry purée. When you eat them slowly a sweet taste explodes in your mouth. This idea comes from many brilliant thoughts on using fruit instead of sugar by writer Elbie Lebrecht.

Garlic

There is a famous recipe for chicken with forty cloves of garlic. The secret is that unpeeled cloves are not that strong. The pungency comes out the more it is chopped, so one cut clove embedded in a casserole will hardly alter the taste, while thin slices inserted in a leg of lamb will. Finely chopped or crushed raw garlic is the most powerful of all.

Herbs

In the USA they are called 'erbs' and the most popular one is 'baysil' (basil). For the best mint tea, you should go to Jerusalem where they serve an infusion of fresh mint leaves. It leaves a clean, fresh taste and helps the digestion. The much-promoted herb teas in packets have less caffeine than normal tea but like decaffeinated coffee, they can have a surprising effect. If you are used to drinking a strong espresso every morning and you suddenly change to decaff, you may get withdrawal symptoms in the form of a ghastly headache.

Ice Cream

The name Häagen–Dazs was chosen by the Americans for their ice cream because they thought a Scandinavian sound would help it to sell. One of their choc ices costs about three weeks' pocket money for most children. If you want to make real vanilla ice cream at home, you can use fresh cream and a vanilla pod and get a similar effect.

Jelly

You can't make pineapple jelly unless you use tinned fruit. Fresh pineapple has an enzyme called bromelin that stops jellies setting and also does something nasty if you mix it with chicken.

Kumquats

These tiny orange-like fruits are exactly the opposite of what you would expect. Unlike their big brother the orange, the skin is sweet and the inside is sour. They make a marvellous preserve to serve with cold meats (see page 183).

Lentils

There are red, green or brown ones. The main difference is that the red ones are used as a thickener since they collapse after about twenty minutes' cooking. The others take about twice as long but keep their round shape. None of them need soaking like beans.

Milk

Milk lasts longer in bottles than cartons. It also tastes slightly better. The other problem with cartons is that people who bite their nails find them hard to open. On the other hand, if you drop a carton on the doorstep you won't have to clear up broken glass. Incidentally, if milk is going sour, pouring it into a cup of hot tea hastens the process. Once it has turned, the best thing to do is to use it for making scones.

Nasturtium

Most flowers are inedible. One that does taste good is the nasturtium with pretty orange and yellow petals and a peppery flavour. To brighten up a salad, you can also try borage which is blue and chive flowers which are lilac. It's best to keep off daffodils and tulips, however pretty they look.

Onions

There are two solutions to the problem of onions making your eyes water. One is to wear swimming goggles while you peel them, but a more practical approach is to stand next to the sink with the cold water running. It certainly stops the tears.

Peaches

In Harry's Bar in Venice they make a drink from white peaches and Prosecco, the Italian version of champagne. They used to have a man who did nothing all day but cut up peaches and squeeze out the juice with his hands. Apparently yellow peaches won't do, nor will a liquidizer. They now import white peach purée from France and I can't help wondering how it's made there.

Quail's Eggs

These taste very similar to hen's eggs – it's the miniature size that makes them attractive. They cook in a minute (the instructions are always on the packs) but are very hard to peel, so if you need a dozen, always buy more.

Red Cabbage

The colours used to describe food are often quite misleading. White grapes are green, blueberries are black and of course red cabbage is purple. When you wash it the water will go blue because of a pigment called anthocyanin. The worst thing about red/purple/blue cabbage is that it has an unpleasant smell when it is cut, so unless it is cooked, it's not a very sociable salad dish.

Sorrel

Recipes for sorrel soup always call for 'handfuls' since it is usually picked locally but it is rarely found in a corner shop. You can buy it packaged in tiny quantities in good supermarkets. A few leaves on top of a small salad add that wonderful after-kick of lemon. Sorrel is also good in tomato sandwiches.

Tomatoes

The acid content in tomatoes has unexpected effects. If you make a soup by adding milk to cooked, puréed tomatoes the mixture will curdle. If you brush meat with a tomato purée-based marinade and cover it with foil, you will find tiny holes in the foil a few hours later.

Unsalted Butter

The pale colour and extra creaminess of unsalted butter makes it more of a delicacy than the yellow, salted version. The salt was originally added to preserve it when few people had fridges. Why adding salt, which is white, turns the butter yellow is a mystery.

Vine Leaves

Packs of grape leaves preserved in brine can be found in delicatessens. In the garden they should be picked early in the year because they get tougher in late summer. Sadly they lose their brilliant green as soon as they are blanched in water but they make the perfect wrapper for rice and any minced meat.

White Raisin (and other Words)

The translation of 'sultana' from English to American becomes 'white raisin'. There are more confusing terms: mature cheddar is rattrap cheese, mackerel is bluefish and aubergines are eggplants. They grind meat instead of mincing it and add scallions instead of spring onions. At least their words don't take on a different meaning according to class. In Britain, dinner is a meal which is eaten in the middle of the day if you're a worker and in the evening if you're an employer.

Xeme

Experts at Scrabble will know that this is "a small black-headed gull of Arctic America having a slightly forked tail." The Arctic Americans probably have a recipe for it too.

Yoghurt

Frozen yoghurt is mistakenly thought to be more healthy than ice cream. Yoghurt of course contains less fat than cream, but because of the higher water content, far more sugar has to be added to make it freeze well. In the same way cereal manufacturers claim proudly that their sugar coated cereals are "low in fat" whereas they should be labelling the boxes "high in sugar".

Zabaglione

This theatrical dessert made from whisking egg yolks to a hot froth with Marsala wine was always popular in Italian restaurants. In spite of the fashion for 'Cal-Ital' food with its Californian overtones, zabaglione is out of favour and the smart fluffy sauce is now French. They call it a 'sabayon', but they make it with champagne.

Jerusalem Artichoke Soup

These knobbly roots — quite unrelated to globe artichokes — have a subtle flavour that is hard to identify but is good in soup. Try to buy large smooth ones as the smaller ones are harder to peel.

½		lemon
1 ½ lbs	700g	Jerusalem artichokes
1-2 tbsp		oil
1		onion
1 pt	600ml	vegetable or chicken stock
For the contrasting watercress purée:		
1 bunch		watercress
2 fl oz	50ml	stock

You will need: a large bowl; a vegetable parer or sharp knife; a saucepan; a liquidizer or food processor and a small dish with a lid for the microwave, or a small saucepan.

Squeeze the lemon and pour the juice into a bowl full of cold water. With a vegetable parer peel the artichokes and cut off any brown ends. Immediately drop them into the acidulated water to stop them going brown.

Chop the onion finely and heat the oil in the saucepan. Sauté the pieces of onion over medium heat, turning them frequently with a spoon so that they stay pale. Drain the artichokes, cut them into chunks and throw them into the saucepan. Season well and pour on the stock, turning up the heat to bring the soup to the boil. When it bubbles, cover it and turn down the heat, leaving it to simmer until the artichokes are tender. They will take about the same time as potatoes, about 15 minutes. While it is cooking prepare the watercress purée. Wash the watercress well, remove the stalks and cook it on **high** in the microwave with the rest of the stock for 1 minute. Alternatively cook it in a small saucepan until it wilts. Purée the soup in one or two batches until it is quite smooth and then pour it back into the saucepan. Pour the cooked watercress and the stock into the liquidizer and blend until it becomes a dark green purée.

Reheat the soup over low heat, pour it into bowls and swirl some of the dark purée into the centre.

Lamb, Lentils and Apricots

The combination of faintly spiced meat and fruit is well known in Morocco but probably unusual elsewhere. The slowly cooked meat can be made early in the day and reheated or even prepared the day before.

2 lb	900g	lean lamb, cut into cubes
2 tbsp		oil
2		large onions
2		large carrots
2 inch	5cm	stick cinnamon (or ½ tsp ground cinnamon)
¼ tsp		turmeric
¼ tsp		chilli powder
I cup		green lentils
12		'no soak' dried apricots

You will need: a casserole with a lid, suitable for a hob and the oven, or a frying pan and a casserole.
Preheat the oven to 350F, 180C, Gas 4.

Cut the peeled onions and carrots into large chunks. Heat the oil in the pan or casserole and sauté them quickly till the onion begins to brown. Take them out and put them on a plate to make room for the meat. Add the cubes of lamb and over medium heat brown them all over, adding a little more oil if necessary and turning frequently so the meat doesn't stick to the bottom. Sprinkle over the spices. Put the vegetables back into the casserole and add the lentils. If you are using a cinnamon stick add it at this stage but don't break it up (you're going to remove it later and it's easier if it's in one piece). Pour three cups of hot water into the casserole, stirring well, and bring it to the boil. Season with a little salt and pepper and transfer it to the oven.

After an hour, check to see that the lentils haven't absorbed all the water, adding another cup if necessary. After another hour the meat should be tender. Press the apricots down into the lamb and lentils and keep the casserole warm for up to twenty minutes. Most of the juices will have been absorbed so it will be fairly dry but if you like some gravy, simply stir in another cup of boiling water. Remove the cinnamon stick and check the seasoning again just before serving.

Boiled or Fried Rice

The makers of pre-processed rice have tried to convince people that cooking ordinary rice is hard. One method – letting the rice absorb an exact quantity of liquid – is tricky. This way, which is the same basic method as for boiling potatoes or pasta, uses plenty of bubbling, salted water, which is then drained. The longer you cook any of these, the softer they get, so the secret is to stop cooking them before they get mushy.

I cup		basmati rice (finer quality than long grain)
I tbsp		sultanas or raisins (optional)
2 tbsp		oil
I inch	2.5cm	cinnamon stick
¼ tsp		turmeric
¼ tsp		tomato purée
I oz	25g	toasted almonds (see page 124)
		salt, pepper

You will need: a large strainer; a large saucepan; a kettle (optional) and a saucer for the microwave (optional).

Put the rice in the strainer and rinse it in cold running water until the water no longer looks cloudy. Half fill the saucepan with boiling water from the kettle (which is quicker than boiling it on the hob), add about a teaspoon of salt and throw in the rice. Stir it, bring the water back to the boil and cook it for 5 – 7 minutes over medium heat. The water should be bubbling all the time and the rice is done when it no longer tastes crunchy. Drain it well through the strainer. At this stage you have perfect boiled rice. The grains should be separate and if you want to finish off the dish later, you should run some cold water through the rice in the strainer and drain it again.

For fried rice, heat the oil in the clean dry saucepan. Add the cinnamon stick and the turmeric (take care when using turmeric not to leave the spoon or any powder on the worksurface as the deep yellow-coloured stain is quite hard to remove). Add the cooked rice, stirring it well to coat all the grains with the flavoured oil. If you are adding sultanas, put them on a saucer with a tablespoon of boiling water, and microwave on **high** for 30 seconds to plump them up. Stir them into the rice with the tomato purée. Taste for seasoning adding pepper and more salt if necessary and remove the cinnamon stick. Pile the fried rice on to a large dish. Scatter over the toasted almonds (adding them earlier will make them go soft) and serve immediately.

Cabbage Leaves Stuffed with Chestnut

This, and the next two recipes, can only be done in the microwave. The leaves are a great accompaniment to roast turkey. They can be prepared in advance and finished off while someone is carving. This recipe makes about 16.

I		green cabbage
I-2 tbsp		oil
I		onion
12 oz	350g	chestnut purée
I oz	25g	toasted cashew nuts
		salt, pepper

You will need: a dish with a cover suitable for the microwave; a shallow glass or china dish; a small frying pan.

Cut a cone out of the base of the cabbage so that the leaves come away and wash them very well. Drain them and microwave half at a time in the covered dish for about I minute on **high** or until they have wilted slightly. Chop the onion and sauté it in the oil until it is golden brown. Stir in a tablespoon of water to deglaze the pan and cook for another minute. Take it off the heat, spoon in the chestnut purée, season well and then fold in the nuts.

Lay out the cabbage leaves and put a heaped spoonful of the chestnut mixture into each one. Roll them up into neat parcels, folding in the edges and making sure the filling is completely enclosed. Arrange them fairly close in a single layer in the shallow dish. The cabbage leaves can be prepared in advance up to this stage.

If they are still warm, cover and reheat them in the microwave on **high** for about a minute. If they have been left to cool it will take about 3 minutes.

Corn on the Cob

I have never tasted sweetcorn as it should be. According to Jane Grigson, you should put a pan of water on the stove to heat up, then go out and cut the cobs. When you buy it, the kernels should be plump even though the hair is dark.

I   corn cob
salt, pepper
as much butter as you like!

This recipe needs no container and no equipment.

Cut off the base to release the outer leaves. Peel them off carefully and wash them. Remove the silky hair. Cover the corn with the damp leaves and put it in the microwave. Cook in its own wrapper on **high** for 3 – 4 minutes. Test to see if it is tender by loosening one or two kernels with a fork, but remember that in general the longer you cook corn the tougher it gets. (Two corn cobs will take about 6 minutes. If you want to cook more, it's better to boil them in a large pan of water.)

Have ready a warm plate and some corn holders if you have any. Sprinkle over plenty of salt and pepper and a large knob of butter.

Spinach Parcels with Peas

The restaurant trick for fresh vegetables is to blanch them in boiling water, leave them to cool and cook them again just before they are served. Thinking along the same lines, these parcels, like the stuffed cabbage, can be prepared early and cooked in minutes while you're serving the main course.

I lb	450g	fresh spinach with large leaves
8 oz	225g	frozen petit pois (small sweeter peas)
		salt, pepper

You will need: a dish with a cover suitable for the microwave; a shallow serving dish with no metal or gold trim and absorbent kitchen paper.

Wash the spinach very well in several changes of cold water. Choose about sixteen of the best, even sized leaves and drain them well. Cook in the covered dish on **high** for 1 minute and then dry them carefully with kitchen paper. Put the peas in the dish and cook, covered on **high** for 1 minute to get rid of any ice. Drain these too.

Spread out the spinach leaves and put a spoonful of peas on to each one. Season with salt and pepper and wrap each one carefully, tucking in the sides and rolling them over. Arrange them in the dish, fairly close together so that the ends are hidden.

When you are ready to eat, cook the parcels on **high** for about 2 minutes and serve them straight away.

Carrot (or Passion) Cake

Vegetables - even courgettes - sometimes turn up unexpectedly in sweet cakes. The original Passion Cake includes walnuts, sultanas and carrots and has a very rich icing. My recipe has a less sweet, sauce-like topping.

10 oz	280g	carrots (about 4)
3 oz	85g	soft brown sugar
4 oz	112g	golden syrup
2 fl oz	56ml	water
4 fl oz	112ml	oil
5 oz	140g	wholemeal flour
6 oz	170g	plain flour
2 tsp		baking powder
½ tsp		mixed spice
2		eggs
For the topping:		
4 oz	112g	ricotta cheese
1 oz	25g	icing sugar

You will need: a grater or food processor; a large glass or china bowl; the microwave or a small saucepan; a strainer; a loose-bottomed cake tin 7 inches (18cm) diameter and 3 inches (8cm) deep. (If you don't have a tin with a removable base you should line the base and sides of the tin with greaseproof paper which can be lifted out with the cake); a palette knife.
Preheat the oven to 350F, 180C, Gas 4.

First grate the carrots finely - either by hand or with the main blade of a food processor. (Don't use the grating disc because it makes coarser pieces.) Melt the sugar with the syrup and water. The easiest way to do this is in a bowl in the microwave. It will take just over a minute on **high**. Stir to make sure the sugar is dissolved. Alternatively, use a saucepan over low heat,so that the mixture doesn't boil, and then transfer it to the bowl. Add the grated carrots and mix in the oil. Then add what is always referred to as 'the dry ingredients'. To make sure there are no lumps, sift the flours and the baking powder through the strainer and stir them into the mixture. Finally add the eggs, beating well to make sure it is smooth.

Brush the inside of the tin with oil to stop the cake sticking and pour in the cake mixture. Level out the top and bake it in the centre of the oven for about 50 minutes. You can tell when it is done if you put a strand of dry spaghetti right down the middle. If it comes out sticky it's not done - otherwise it is. Take the cake out and leave it in the tin to cool slightly - at least fifteen minutes. Then ease round the edge with a knife and carefully push up the base.

Leave the cake to cool and then make the topping. Press the ricotta through a strainer and then mix it with the icing sugar. Serve it in a small bowl with the cake or spoon some over the top.

Strawberries with Orange Juice

Summer strawberries have a sweetness and flavour that needs no additions. The firm imported ones that appear in the shops in winter need a little help.

1 lb	450g	strawberries
1		large orange
1-2 tbsp		sugar

You will need: a bowl; a strainer and clingfilm.

Wash and hull the strawberries and if they are large cut them up. Arrange them in a glass bowl. Cut the orange in half and squeeze the juice into a cup. Sprinkle the strawberries with a little sugar, then strain over the orange juice. Cover with film and refrigerate until about an hour before you serve them.

The Menu

Herb Flower Pots

Smoked Salmon Fishes

Liver Pâté with Pistachios and Quail's Eggs

French Bean Sheaves

Courgette Curls

• • •

Orange Salad with Satsuma Flowers

Caramel Circles

Mangos

Melon Basket

Carved Watermelon

Ice Flower Bowl

The Techniques

Cutting, carving and gardening

It's Looking Good

On the morning of a State Banquet at Windsor Castle a team of footmen will begin to polish the long mahogany table. It stretches the length of eight London buses and is so wide that it needs one person wielding a duster on each side while a third slides backwards on protective kneepads along the centre. Every piece of porcelain is checked. Each glass and silver gilt spoon must shine. A hundred and sixty chairs are checked with a ruler, one by one, to make sure they are all the same distance from the table. The Queen, of course, has different standards from most of her subjects but even she acknowledges that bringing out the Mecklenburgh dinner service is not something they do every day.

Whenever we eat with friends we adopt a more formal style, even if it just means that we set the table instead of eating our food from a tray in front of television. At home it often seems an effort to make the food taste good, let alone worry about fiddly decoration to make it look good. There are two quite different approaches to the way food should look. First there is the decorative look. In Escoffier's time, a French-trained chef would never have succeeded without knowing how to embed a sliced truffle in aspic. Starred restaurants today still feature desserts covered with a spun sugar cage and a feathered trail of piped white chocolate on a pool of red sauce.

As a reaction against such perfection, many people prefer the second approach. Food should look abundant and unadorned. At grand parties, waiters will pass round enormous perspex trays arranged with a single choice of unglazed canapés in well-spaced rows. At the side of the room will be wheelbarrows full of baby vegetables and hollowed out cabbages filled with taramasalata and hummus.

Yet the comment "I hate fussy food" can be a smokescreen for not bothering to make the best of anything. Carving vegetables to look like flowers is one extreme – serving some stale cheese on a chipped plate is the other. In the middle is what most people would choose; using a bit of imagination to make simple food look great.

Advertisements encourage the connection in our minds between the look and taste of food. The mouthwatering photographs we see on hoardings are designed to make us buy the product. How is it that yoghurt topped with a single strawberry can look so perfect? Most people believe that the food is tampered with and not quite what it seems. This is far from the truth for what makes a perfect shot is not deception but hours of expensive professional time. The strawberry is first chosen from a box of fifty and the other forty-nine are discarded. Photographers, designers and stylists work for hours to prepare the backdrop and the lighting. Then the home economist arrives. This title used to refer to someone who taught cookery in schools. Now it means someone armed with a fine brush and a pair of tweezers, who adds a gloss of oil to one perfect leaf. With a background of jazz chosen from a shelf of CDs, the team sips wine and examines the polaroids under a magnifying glass. After four hours they will have achieved one perfect photograph.

The link between the eye and the palate is so strong that a dish will not look appealing if you don't think it's going to taste good. A pile of honeydew melon slices dotted with blackberries and dark plums makes a good ending to a September meal. A bowl of frigid looking strawberries with green and white tips in January has far less appeal. In the same way no amount of decoration will make fish fingers as tempting as a plate of sizzling barbecued spare ribs.

Yet imagination can help. A bunch of grapes on a plate may not look like a centrepiece. Presented in another way it will. Cover a flat tray with fig leaves from the garden, choose a bunch of huge muscat grapes in season and lay them on top, sprinkling over some drops of icy water to keep them looking fresh. Simple flowers can be treated in the same way. Instead of spending money on costly arrangements, you can fill a glass decanter with water and push down some tiny flowers like lobelia or lily of the valley, before replacing the lid. You can even tint the water slightly with a dash of food colouring. Don't worry if there are no flowers at all. A long flat tray covered with red tinged autumn leaves and shiny conkers looks better than wilting rosebuds. Another idea for a plain tablecloth or wood surface is an arrangement of vegetables – pink fir-apple potatoes, red chillies, a bunch of beetroot with the leaves on or baby artichokes.

On festive occasions we spend a fortune on silver ornaments and crackers containing feeble jokes. A better idea to get people talking is to save cartoons or 'quotes of the week' and put one at each place, wrapped in a square of shiny coloured paper and tied with narrow metallic ribbon. If you have access to a photocopier you can have fun with newspaper headlines. On a momentous occasion like a peace-signing or a political landslide you can reduce the size of the paper with its headline until it is still readable but about four inches long. It takes several goes, and much wasted paper, but when you have reached the final miniature size, you can duplicate that for each guest. Then roll it up and tie it with red wool or ribbon. If you're celebrating a birthday or an engagement you can even insert a photo of the star guest and make your own headline with letraset. An imaginative bit of fun like this is more likely to be remembered than the grandest array of silver and starched linen.

The opponents of decoration claim that it takes too long. Certainly it takes a while to make roses out of spirals of thinly cut tomato skin, but it takes no longer to turn a mango into pretty raised chunks than to peel it and make slices. Of course, some artistry is done by professionals, like chefs who turn slabs of butter or ice into sculptures. But it only needs an eye for colour to work out that tomatoes don't look good with beetroot.

One of the most impressive edible tricks I ever saw was at a wedding. The bride carried a bouquet of white lilies. A few of the same lilies cascaded down the side of the three-tiered cake. The petals were almost transparent and it was clear that the florist had used the same flowers to decorate the cake. It turned out that those lilies were made entirely of sugar – an unbelievable masterpiece.

The ideas for the menu in this chapter are what you might call fiddly/ridiculous/fun or brilliant. If you're inclined to tick either of the first two adjectives, but still fancy causing a slight stir at your table, the first recipe is for you. The rest are all for people who like to play with their food.

Herb Flower Pots

The joke presentation of this starter for six people is that it looks like a gardener's prizewinning entry.

2 quantities	Almond, Onion and Mushroom Pâté (page 18)
	small iceberg lettuce
	growing herbs: chives, chervil or rosemary
1	courgette
	some cherry tomatoes

You will need: 6 small plastic flower pots; a one inch paper rosette with the words '1st Prize' written across it and a few pins.

Make up the pâté (recipe on page 18) doubling the quantities. Shred the lettuce and spoon a little into the base of each flower pot. When the pâté has cooled, divide it into six and scoop it on top of the lettuce. Press a long stemmed herb into each one, so that it looks as if it is growing in the pot. Rosemary is best because it stands very straight, but chives or chervil will do if you put them in at the last moment – otherwise they will wilt. Arrange the pots in the middle of the table with a pile of cherry tomatoes. Pin the rosette on to the courgette, so that it looks like a miniature marrow.

Smoked Salmon Fishes

When a tray of mixed sandwiches is passed round, most of us would choose the smoked salmon, leaving all the egg ones for someone else. This is a way of making a small number look good. It makes 8 open sandwiches in the shape of a fish and a few closed ones, using the bits which are left. If you don't have a special cutter, you can make the shape out of paper.

4 oz	112g	smoked salmon
8 slices		brown bread (medium thickness)
1 oz	25g	butter
1		lemon

Using the cutter or a piece of paper shaped like a fish, make 8 fish shapes about 3 inches (8cm) long, using about 4 slices of bread. Spread the smoked salmon out in one layer and make 8 equal sized shapes. You will need to use a knife as well since cutters are not usually sharp enough to go through something slippery like smoked salmon. Butter the bread and arrange the salmon on top. Cut the lemon into wedges and arrange them on a flat plate with the salmon fishes. To use up the remaining bits, cut the rest of the bread into very small rounds or squares, butter them generously and put in the smoked salmon. Cover the plates with foil or clingfilm and refrigerate until about half an hour before you serve them.

Liver Pâté with Pistachios and Quail's Eggs

There's a lot in a name. Chopped liver is simply chopped liver, the best known of all Jewish appetisers. A 'terrine' conjures up the image of exotic French pâté and requires an oven, and long cooking in a bain marie. Here is a recipe that looks like the second, with the speed and simplicity of the first.

8 oz	225g	chicken livers
1		large onion
3 tbsp		oil
3 tbsp		chicken stock
2 oz	50g	pistachio nuts (shelled)
		salt, pepper
6		quail's eggs

You will need: a non-stick pan; a small saucepan; a food processor or liquidizer and some tinfoil.

Peel the onion and chop it finely. Heat the oil in the frying pan and sauté the chopped onion until it is light brown. Add the chicken livers and turn them frequently until they are brown on all sides. Season with salt and pepper and then pour in the chicken stock. Turn down the heat and cook for a minute or two. Spoon the livers into a blender, season with salt and pepper and buzz for a minute, or until you have a smooth pâté. While it is cooling, hard boil the quail's eggs following the instructions on the pack. Peel the eggs carefully and slice them in half lengthwise when they have cooled. Divide the pâté into portions and form each one into a rectangle about a centimetre thick. Make a slight indentation in the centre and press in the halved egg, making it level with the top of the pâté. Halve the pistachios and press a few into each portion too, with the cut green side up.

If you don't want to serve it straight away, leave out the eggs and freeze the pâté, spreading it out on to a double thickness of foil. Form it into one large rectangle, press in the halved pistachio nuts and mark it into equal sized squares. Open freeze until it is firm and then store covered. To serve, lift the frozen squares on to individual plates and leave to defrost for about an hour. (Don't try to lift them off once they have softened.)

French Bean Sheaves

If you've done everything you can for a special dinner and happen to have fifteen minutes spare, here are a couple of ideas to pass the time while you wait for the doorbell to ring.

8 oz	225g	french beans
I		leek

You will need: a shallow dish for the microwave and a sheet of clingfilm (no alternative because they will collapse in water).

Wash and trim the beans and cut them into even lengths. Arrange them in piles of about four or five. Cut down the length of the leek with a sharp knife, so that the outer layers open out. Wash a few of these and microwave them on **high** for 20 seconds so that they are no longer stiff. Cut them into long, very thin strips, about the thickness of a strand of wool and use these to wrap the beans into bundles. You can either make a bow or just tie a small knot. Arrange the sheaves on the dish in a single layer, sprinkle over a few tablespoons of salted water, and cover with clingfilm.

When you are ready to serve the main course, microwave the beans on **high** for 3 minutes, drain off the water and serve immediately.

Courgette Curls

I	courgette

You will need: a vegetable parer and some cocktail sticks.

Wash the courgette and cut off the ends. Holding the vegetable parer, pull it down the length of the courgette making a very thin slice with edges of dark skin. Continue making slices till you have used up the courgette. It should make about ten. Roll up each slice fairly tightly and keep them firmly rolled by passing a cocktail stick through the centre. You can fit two or three on one stick, but leave a gap for the air to circulate. Arrange the finished curls on a plate and microwave on **high** for 30 seconds. Leave them to cool slightly, slide them off the sticks and use as a decoration for vegetables or a salad.

Orange Salad with Satsuma Flowers

Satsuma 'flowers' are not what you might imagine. They are simply halved fruit cut in a way that reveals the bright juicy centre rather than the dull, skinny outside. You might like to add a dash of cointreau, but since my first introduction to a gin-soaked orange salad in my teens, I have preferred to enjoy alcohol and fruit separately.

Quantities for each person:

1	large juicy orange
1	satsuma
	sugar (depending on the sweetness of the fruit)

You will need: a large flat plate; a sharp, serrated knife and a glass bowl for serving.

To peel oranges for a salad you need to remove the skin and the white pith. The easiest way to do this is to slice off each end and then stand the orange up vertically. Cut the skin off downwards, turning the orange round and making sure you remove the inner layer of transparent skin too. It's quite hard to get this right first time, since you either seem to be removing too much or too little. Take care not to lose the juice and then cut the peeled oranges into thin slices and put them in the bowl with the juice. Sprinkle over a little sugar if you like. Peel the satsumas with your hands, removing the little white strings that cling to the skin inside. Then simply cut them horizontally in half so that each half looks like a flower. Arrange the satsumas on top of the oranges, with the cut side uppermost. Cover the bowl with clingfilm and refrigerate the salad till about half an hour before you serve it.

Caramel Circles

These look like stained glass and are not difficult to make. The method is the same as for the caramel in Stuffed Dates (page 106).

8 oz	225g	granulated sugar
3 fl oz	75ml	water (about half a cup)
I tbsp		oil

You will need: a small saucepan; several sheets of foil and a spoon with a long handle.

Lay the foil on the work surface and brush over a thin film of oil. Make the caramel according to the instructions on page 106, omitting the liquid glucose. When it starts to boil, keep watching it and when the thick bubbles begin to turn golden it is nearly ready. It can turn dark brown in thirty seconds, and actually continues to cook slightly off the heat.

Dip the spoon into the caramel and quickly swirl some caramel on to the foil to make a circle. Keep doing this, leaving some space in between each one. Work quickly as the caramel will get darker and begin to set in a few minutes. It doesn't matter if some of the caramel trails round the edges of the circles - it even looks nicer. Leave them to cool completely and then slide your fingers along underneath the foil to release each circle. Store them on a fresh sheet of foil, in the fridge, or covered in a container. They can be served with the orange salad, or can be used to decorate a cake. (Pipe some whipped cream over a sponge cake and press some caramel circles round the edge, so that they stand up.)

Mangos

The best, or the worst, thing about mangos (depending on whether you like or loathe them) is the perfume.

- For sliced mangos: Peel half the fruit and cut across it with a sharp knife. Then turn it round and do the same with the other side. Some of the flesh will stick to the flat stone in the middle, so eat it when no-one is looking, but the fibres stick in your teeth so make sure you have a toothpick.
- For halved mangos: Stand the mango up and with a sharp knife cut through the skin to within about half an inch of the centre. Turn it round and do the same on the other side, leaving the long flat stone surrounded by a strip of skin and some of the flesh. On the cut sides, make two or three horizontal cuts and then make vertical cuts to form squares. The cuts should go almost down to the skin. Lift up each half and press the skin gently from underneath. The mango will open out and form what looks like a carved dome.

Melon Basket

A surprising way of serving a large melon is to bring it to the table looking whole, when you have actually cut it into a basket shape.

You will need: a sharp knife; a melon baller (optional); a spoon and a pencil.

Stand the melon up vertically and cut off the more pointed end to make a flat base. Starting in the middle of the melon, draw a line over the top slightly to the side of the centre ending in the middle on the other side. Turn the melon round and draw a parallel line just the other side of the centre. Cut along the lines forming a strip about half an inch wide. This is going to be the handle. Now make a scalloped pattern round the side of the melon (you can also do this with a pencil first) and cut deeply through the skin until you reach the line of the handle at the other side. Take care not to cut across this line and make a similar pattern on the other side. It doesn't matter if the scallops are even – you just have to end the last one so that it meets the line of the handle. Go round the pattern again, cutting a little deeper and then carefully lift out the two side pieces. The basket is nearly finished, but you have to remove the solid piece of melon under the handle, so cut it away leaving the skin in place. Scoop out the seeds from the middle with a large spoon before you reassemble it to bring to table. Or, make melon balls and fill the basket with them.

Carved Watermelon

In Bangkok every fruit and vegetable is carved with intricate patterns. If you are artistic you can take a small sharp knife and carve flowers, a face or a geometric pattern into the dark green waxy skin to show the pale green inside. (If you go much deeper you will come to the bright red layer.)

Ice Flower Bowl

If you're still reading this chapter, the chances are that you haven't dismissed the occasional decorative touch as a waste of time. The final dish needs no ingredients – just water and a garden (or even a patio or windowbox if you live in town). This is a dish in the container sense of the word. It is a bowl made of ice embedded with blossom or flowers.

You will need: two heavy glass bowls of slightly different sizes and some stickytape; v ery small petals or flowers like fuchsia or lobelia; tiny leaves or fern.

Pour a little boiled and cooled water into the space between the two bowls – about enough to cover the bottom. Press some flowers and greenery right down so that they stay under the water. Fix the two bowls firmly together by sticking the tape across the top. Put them in the freezer until the water is turning to ice. Then pour in some more water and press some more flowers down to fill up the space between the bowls. Move them around so that they look good. Put the double bowl in the freezer and freeze the water until it is absolutely hard. Now comes the tricky part. Pour a little warm water into the top glass bowl and wiggle it carefully until the bowl comes away from the ice. Stand the other bowl in some more warm water and gently ease the flower embedded ice bowl away.

Now it probably won't work the first time. It's very likely to crack or break. Remember that most skills need practice, so don't be disappointed and give it another try. Next time you will be really pleased when you are standing there with a perfect bowl, made of ice and flowers. You can now put it in the freezer – carefully wrapped – and bring it out when strawberries are in season.

The Menu

Sandwiches

Scones

Date Bread

Ginger Cake

Crème Pâtissière

Strawberry Cream Sponge Cake

Blueberry Pancakes

Pecan Butter Whirls

The Techniques

More baking

Light sponge cake

Thick pancakes

Pastries

Time for Tea

Afternoon tea in Eaton Square was a daily ritual at the turn of the century. Letters of invitation, posted before breakfast, would arrive at noon – neat embossed cards with the words 'At Home'– five o'clock.

In the Upstairs Downstairs world of silver teapots and fine china, preparations began early. The cook was in charge of the baking. Scullery maids were busy clearing the breakfast and preparing a layered meat galantine for the family lunch. The second kitchenmaid made the dough for crumpets and currant buns and then set to work making scotch pancakes and scones – merely the starters on the tea menu. The kitchen filled with steam, for without a freezer everything was freshly made each day. By four o'clock the tiered cake stands were in place – a walnut layer cake with sweet butter cream perched above plates of brandy snaps, madeleines and parkin.

The women guests far outnumbered the men and their conversation centred on the other social events that filled their diaries. They didn't stay long and often flitted from one formal tea to another, making sure they left enough time to be home and dressed for dinner at eight. Whether they left enough room to cope with soup, fish, a roast and a pudding is another question.

Tea as a meal has now virtually disappeared. The vast amounts of food consumed in those times is viewed today with amusement and some horror. Is there a danger that the pleasure of sipping a hot drink and eating a single pastry will eventually disappear too? Drinking tea or coffee on its own is acceptable at any hour of the day, but the diet-conscious western world has made cake a forbidden word. Whenever a hand reaches out for a cream bun you can be sure to hear the comment "I shouldn't really" as the fork goes in. Perhaps teatime should be renamed 'the guilty hour'. It could come as a prelude to the American 'happy hour' when half-price cocktails are consumed before dinner.

Comedians take full advantage of our paranoia: "Diets are for those who are thick and tired of it" or "I've been on a diet for the last two decades. I've lost so much weight I should be hanging from a charm bracelet."

The crime of eating sweet concoctions has always been prevalent. In France and Italy it seems to go on in secret, at home. In the cafés the natives drink strong coffee and read the newspapers while the waiters offer the cake menu to the tourists. The Spaniards, on the other hand, indulge their sweet tooth at almost any hour of the day or evening. Starting with fried churros at eleven in the morning, they eat cakes with the children at the six o'clock merienda and enjoy huge trays of almond pastries and profiteroles on Sundays after mass.

Women seem to enjoy cakes and pastries even more than men. My own weakness is not just the eating, but the looking as well. Most of my friends would be happy window shopping for clothes. My greatest pleasure on holiday is wandering across cobbled streets to gaze into the window of every single pâtisserie in the town. In Italy there are puffy doughnuts called bomboloni, filled with vanilla custard. In France every cake has a name, but you don't need a dictionary to understand the labels: a sacristain, a religieuse and a financier; a diplomate, a japonais and a marquis. Whoever thought of calling a gâteau after Richelieu and Napoleon or decreeing that a folded puff pastry has to be called a jalousie?

In England the baker's shop is a disappointment. Old recipe books describe exciting things like stuffed monkey and fat rascals but the cakes on sale are probably oversized scones or sticky Danish pastries. You have to go into the country to find a real English tea and it probably won't be in a four star hotel. In Devon there is a small farmhouse with a sign that says "Historic House – Cream Teas". The owners are in the process of restoring a tumbledown cottage. The staircase is dangerously rickety and the upstairs rooms have falling plaster and some rusty farm implements as exhibits. Somehow they get away with charging an entrance fee to view these relics but they are forgiven because of the tea they serve in the basement kitchen. A couple of persian cats lounge under the large table, warming themselves near the old but not antique, cooker. The cream tea arrives – a huge pot of Indian tea and a pile of warm scones. On the tray is a generous bowl of thick clotted cream and none of those horrid portion-controlled packs of red jam, but a jar of thick strawberry conserve with whole berries.

At the centre of English tea at home is the birthday cake. My attempts at children's party cakes involved more imagination than skill. I produced a pink panther, a Red Indian complete with feathers and a chocolate humpty dumpty egg sitting on an edible wall. But icing these brilliant designs turned out to be a nightmare. I was hopeless at smoothing and piping. Trying to reproduce a filofax recently I discovered the solution: ready-to-roll fondant which can just be lifted on to the cake. This would have been unbelievable news for the cook in 1871 who was given this advice on how to ice a very large cake:

"Beat the whites of twenty eggs, by degrees, in a pound of double refined sugar; mix these well in a deep earthenware pan; add enough orange flower water, and a piece of lemon peel; whisk it for three hours, till the mixture is thick and white; then, with a thin, broad bit of board, spread it over the top and sides, and set it in a cool oven; an hour will harden it".

One of the quickest tea time treats comes from Boston, the home of the original tea party. A pile of blueberry pancakes can be made in a quarter of an hour. The recipe makes me smile because it reminds me of how we obtained the huge bag of blueberries in the freezer. My youngest son went on his own, at the age of ten, to visit his brother in America. Travelling as an 'unaccompanied minor' he wore a large name tag and was looked after by a charming stewardess at both ends of the journey. Having tasted blueberry muffins and pancakes covered in maple syrup he decided to bring some berries home as a present for us. In the seat next to him was a businessman and for six hours they discussed his purchase and the dilemma that faced him. Did he have to declare the berries to the Customs official in London? He couldn't have been more worried if he'd been carrying a parcel of drugs. At Heathrow he walked through the green channel and proudly presented us with his illegal gift.

Making tea at home is the easiest way to entertain a dozen friends on a Sunday afternoon. Most people don't have a giant roast for lunch so you can be sure they'll be hungry. All you need to do is provide something savoury, something sweet and some tea. When the drink was first introduced in the American colonies, they didn't know what to do with it and served the leaves with sugar or syrup and threw away the water they'd been boiled in. Today you can offer anything from a thick brew made from round or square tea bags to a mild infusion of Earl Grey or jasmine flowers.

To start with it's a good idea to have a plate of sandwiches. Marks and Spencer have realised that busy people don't want to be buttering bread before they leave for work in the morning. The weekday sandwich business has become so competitive that they consult weather experts to determine how many prawn and how many chicken tikka sandwiches to make for the following day. There are however, some sandwiches which are easy to make at home and don't come in a triangular plastic pack.

As for the sweet things, you can serve just one or two items. If you're playing safe you can stick to an apple pie and a plate of chocolate brownies, which you've probably mastered already. In this chapter there are recipes for some more cakes, including the famous light sponge cake that was the basis of my early successes (and disasters). There are no complicated chocolate éclairs or six layered dobostorte, but to make sure the cakes work, do measure the ingredients carefully and use the right size tin. Have a nice tea.

Sandwiches

In the thirties 'high tea' often included meat sandwiches with tongue or liver sausage or a savoury like sardines on toast. The sandwiches to eat while lounging around with the Sunday papers can be much lighter. Here are some ideas for fillings, which are not expensive, and are mostly suitable for vegetarians. They can be made with hefty wedges of granary bread, or elegant fingers of thinly-sliced white.

- Peel and slice some tomatoes, dry them well with paper towels and add a few leaves of rocket or sorrel for extra bite.

- Thinly slice some radishes and arrange them on a bed of fresh watercress leaves.

- Cover the bread with mascarpone cheese instead of butter and add some strips of red pepper.

- A thin layer of smoked cod's roe makes an unusual and salty contrast to bland slices of well-drained cucumber.

- Mash some hard-boiled eggs with a spoonful of plain yoghurt and a few anchovy fillets.

- Greek taramasalata and sliced black olives make a pretty and piquant filling.

- A few flakes of cold poached salmon mixed with mayonnaise makes a more substantial sandwich.

- If you're not bothering with cakes, a few sweet fillings can be included. Cream cheese and fresh dates is one idea; another is clotted cream and sliced strawberries.

Scones

To bake a batch of scones takes 8 - 10 minutes in a hot oven. They are best eaten the same day but you can make them in advance and freeze them. This amount makes about 10.

8 oz	250g	self raising flour
I level tsp		baking powder
½ oz	15g	sugar
5 fl oz	125ml	fresh or soured milk
I oz	25g	butter
To serve with them:		
		thick or clotted cream
		blackcurrant, raspberry or strawberry jam

You will need: a bowl; a strainer; a baking sheet; a rolling pin and a round cutter or a small glass.
Preheat the oven to 450F, 225C, Gas 8.

Mix the baking powder with the flour. Shake it through a strainer, partly to get rid of any lumps and also to make it lighter. With your fingers rub in the butter and then stir in the sugar. The mixture should be crumbly. Add the milk and stir quickly until the mixture comes together into a ball. Sprinkle a little more flour on to a board and knead the dough briefly. Don't work it too much, it just needs to be smooth. Use the rolling pin to level the surface so that it is about 1 inch(2.5cm) thick. Dip the cutter or glass in some flour and pr ess it down into the dough to make rounds. Alternatively you can simply cut it into squares. You can reform the dough that is left to make a few morescones. Ar range them on a lightly greased baking tray and brush the tops with a little milk. Bake for about 10 – 12 minutes.

When they are cooked the scones will have risen and should be light brown on top. Leave them to cool and then pull them in half (cutting with a knife toughens them), before you butter them. If there are any left, store them overnight in a polythene bag. To restore the freshness or to use defrosted scones, arrange them on a plate and microwave on **high** for between 10 (for one) and 40 seconds (for two or three).

Date Bread

A sweet loaf with no sugar, that can be thinly sliced and buttered. The bread takes minutes to put together and when cooked will freeze or keep for a few days.

8 oz	230g	stoned dried dates in a packet
½ tsp		bicarbonate of soda
5 fl oz	150ml	boiling water
1		egg
½ oz	15g	butter
5 oz	150g	self-raising flour
To serve:		
		lightly salted or unsalted butter

You will need: a sharp knife; a bowl; a loaf tin (1 lb/450g capacity or measuring 8"×4"×3"/20 × 10 × 8cm); greaseproof paper and some oil for greasing; an electric mixer (optional); a long cocktail stick or a piece of raw spaghetti.
Preheat the oven to 325F, 160C, Gas 3.

Cut the slab of dried dates downwards into thin slices and put the broken up pieces in the bowl with the soda and boiling water. Leave the dates to soak for about five minutes.

Meanwhile cut a rectangle of paper about 16" × 12" (40 × 30cm) and brush it with oil on both sides. Press it into the tin making diagonal cuts at the corners to make it fit neatly, taking care that there are no holes for the mixture to seep through.

With an electric mixer or a large spoon, beat the egg, sugar, butter and flour in with the softened dates until the mixture is smooth. There will be a few pieces of date but there shouldn't be any lumps of flour. Pour it into the lined tin and bake for about an hour. Test to see if the centre is done by inserting a stick and if it comes out dry, take the bread out of the oven. Leave it to cool a little and then lift it out of the tin. When it is cold, carefully remove the paper. To store it, wrap the loaf in foil or clingfilm.

Ginger Cake

Another cake which is quick to prepare but takes time to cook. It is even better made in advance so that the flavour can mature. If you have any left over it can be served as a dessert with custard and a halved ripe pear.

3 oz	85g	unsalted butter
3 oz	85g	molasses or brown sugar
5 tbsp		golden syrup
8 oz	225g	self raising flour
¼ tsp		bicarbonate of soda
I flat tsp		powdered ginger
5 fl oz	150ml	milk
I		egg

You will need: a loaf tin (same size as for the date bread and lined with oiled greaseproof paper in the same way); a large bowl; a hand or electric whisk; a saucepan (if you have no microwave); a strainer and a sheet of foil.
Preheat the oven to 350F, 180C, Gas 4.

Grease and line the loaf tin before you start to make the cake. In the microwave melt the butter, sugar and syrup together. This will take about 2 minutes on **high** in a large uncovered bowl. Alternatively use a pan over very low heat. Don't let the mixture boil. Sift the flour, soda and ginger through a strainer into another bowl. Mix the egg with the milk, using a fork or whisk. Now mix everything together until you have a smooth mixture with no lumps. The easiest way to do this is to slide some of the flour into the warm sugar mixture and beat in half the liquid, then continue stirring and add the rest.

Pour the cake mixture in to the tin and bake for about 45 minutes. To see if it is done, it should be well risen and a stick or skewer inserted into the middle should come out dry. Leave it to cool in the tin. Then take it out, peel off the paper and wrap the cake in foil. If you can resist eating it for a few days, you will find that the flavour improves.

Crème Pâtissière (or Custard)

Cooking egg yolks over direct heat is considered tricky because they can so easily curdle or turn the mixture into something which looks like scrambled eggs. Adding some flour stops this happening so it's as easy to make this custard as to make up the yellow powder that comes out of a packet.

2		egg yolks
I tbsp		vanilla sugar
I tbsp		plain flour
½ pt	300ml	milk

You will need: a cup or glass; a small saucepan; a strainer and a jug.

Break the eggs, one at a time, and drop the whites into a cup. (Keep these, covered in the fridge, for something else.) Rinse out the saucepan with cold water but don't dry it. This helps to stop the milk sticking. Mix the egg yolks in the saucepan with the sugar and flour until it looks like a paste.

Pour in the milk and stir over medium heat for about three minutes. At this stage it will begin to thicken. Keep stirring all the time and a minute later it will have turned into custard. Strain it into the jug to get rid of any small lumps and leave it to get cold. If you want it to cool quickly, stand the jug in cold water (not under a dripping tap) or by an open window.

Strawberry Cream Sponge Cake

To make a successful sponge cake you need to whisk in a lot of air. Heating the bowl and sifting the flour helps, but using an electric beater is the real solution.

5		large eggs
5 oz	150g	sugar
4½ oz	130g	self raising flour
½ pt	300ml	whipping or double cream
8 oz	225g	strawberries
		butter or oil to grease the tins

You will need: 2 round 8 inch (20cm) tins (preferably with removable bases or some greaseproof paper to line them); a large bowl; an electric whisk; a strainer and a spatula.
Preheat the oven to 425F, 220C, Gas 7.

Grease the tins, and, if the bases are not removable, line them with greased paper. Warm the bowl with hot water and then, making sure it is quite dry, whisk together the eggs and the sugar until they are pale yellow and fluffy. This will take several minutes with an electric whisk and about ten or more with an exhausted arm and a hand whisk. Sift the flour and sprinkle a little on to the egg mixture. Fold it in gently with a spatula and keep adding more, turning the mixture over until there are no trails of dry flour. The idea is to keep in the air, while making sure that the flour is well incorporated.

Spoon the mixture into the prepared cake tins and bake in the centre of the oven for about 12 minutes. The cake is done when it begins to come away from the edges of the tin. A cocktail stick inserted in the centre should come out dry. Leave for a few minutes and then carefully take the cakes out of the tin and let them cool on some greaseproof paper or a wire rack.

Whisk the cream in a chilled bowl until it is thick. Take care not to go on too long. Wash the strawberries and dry them well with paper towels. Cut them in halves or slices. Pile half the cream on to one cake and spread it out. Arrange half the strawberries on top and cover with the other cake. Spoon on the rest of the cream, spreading it out to the edge. Arrange the remaining strawberries round the top and keep the cake cool until you are ready to serve it.

Blueberry Pancakes

The batter used for these pancakes is thicker than the one for crêpes, which contains more liquid. As a result they don't spread so much and can hold the berries while they cook. It's best to serve them hot but they can be kept warm for about five minutes until they are all ready. If you don't have any blueberries, don't worry. You can serve them with a dollop of butter and call them drop scones or Scotch pancakes.

5 oz	150g	plain flour
1 heaped tsp		baking powder
2		eggs
1 tbsp		vanilla sugar
6 fl oz	170ml	milk
5 oz	150g	blueberries
		oil for greasing the pan
To serve:		
		maple syrup or butter

You will need: paper towels; a bowl; a strainer; a griddle or heavy flat frying pan; a palette knife and greaseproof paper.

Put the berries in the strainer and rinse them quickly. Dry them very well with paper towels. Make sure the strainer is quite dry too. Sift the flour and the baking powder into the bowl. Add the eggs, sugar and a little milk and stir to mix them all together. Beat quite vigorously to get rid of the lumps and then stir in the rest of the milk. When the batter is smooth add the blueberries.

Oil the griddle very lightly and when it is hot spoon some of the batter into small heaps, not too close together. The mixture will start to set immediately and small bubbles will appear on the surface. Slide the palette knife underneath and quickly flip them over. Cook the other side for a shorter time and arrange the cooked pancakes on the greaseproof paper. Continue till you have used up all the batter, but don't pile them on top of each other. To keep the pancakes warm, lay them out on a flat dish in a very low oven (250F, 130C, Gas 1/2).

Pecan Butter Whirls

These are the cheat's Danish pastries. Instead of using a yeast dough that takes hours, the technique is like making puff pastry by rolling and folding. Though the instructions are long, it sounds much harder than it is.

8 oz	225g	self-raising flour
5 oz	140g	soft butter
5 fl oz	150ml	milk
3 tbsp		granulated sugar
1 - 2 tbsp		pecan nuts, chopped
2 oz	50g	icing sugar

You will need: a mixing bowl; a very large baking tin or two smaller ones; a palette knife and a rolling pin.
Preheat the oven to 350F, 180C, Gas 4.

Put the flour into the bowl and rub in 2oz (50g) butter until the mixture is crumbly. Add the milk and mix to a firm dough. Sprinkle a little flour over the board or worksurface and roll the dough into a rectangle.

With a knife, make two faint horizontal lines to mark it out into three equal parts. Spread half the remaining butter (one and a half ounces /45g) over the top two-thirds of the pastry and sprinkle over a tablespoon of sugar. With a palette knife, fold the unbuttered portion up, and the top buttered portion over, making a smaller rectangle containing three layers. Turn the dough at right angles and roll it out again, away from you, to make a long strip about 5" × 18" (12.5 × 45 cm). Spread the rest of the butter all over this piece and dot it with chopped pecann uts. Sprinkle over the rest of the granulated sugar. Then roll the dough sideways like a long swiss roll and cut it into thick slices (1"/2.5cm). Arrange these, cut side up, on a greased baking sheet. Make sure they are not too close together as they spread during the cooking. Bake for about 25 minutes or until they are light brown.

To finish the pastries, lift them off the tin with the palette knife straight away and leave them to cool on a wire rack or a sheet of greaseproof paper. (If you wait they may stick and the tin will be harder to wash.) Mix the icing sugar with a tablespoon of water until it forms a glossy icing and brush this over the tops of the pastries.

Getting Ahead

This chapter has no menu as it is a preparation for your feast. It contains recipes that can all be done early – a month, a week or just before the great day. These include a couple of easy starters, a stunning dessert and some fruit preserves to go with cold meats.

I have never classified recipes as easy or hard but would rather tell you which ones are quick or long. You've now learnt all the techniques needed to make everything in the book, so if you see a long description, you will know that it is not necessarily complicated.

You might prefer to get ahead using ideas from earlier chapters. Soups and casseroles often improve overnight; many pâtés, cakes and pastries come to no harm if they are frozen or cooked the day before.

I once read a piece of advice about planning a dinner party. "Make sure that two days before, you put clean towels in the bathroom." Unless you live alone (and even then, you must need to wipe your hands) this is plainly ridiculous. There are far better things to be doing before a party. I agree it will take longer than looking for clean linen, but you might try the amazing soufflé-filled pancakes on page 178. Every single step is done in advance and they go straight from the freezer, into the oven and on to the table.

At the beginning of this book I promised that by the end you would be able to invite anyone you know to a marvellous meal. If you can present them with something surprisingly good, you will have succeeded in making a feast. The meal doesn't need to be enormous. You can choose from the recipes in these final two chapters to make a feast of any size: an intimate lunch or dinner, or by adding more dishes, a brunch or supper party.

Preparing for The Feast

Most cookbooks – regardless of the words in the title – are about entertaining. The aim of every recipe writer is to explain how to get food together and present it to someone else. Even books on one subject, like soup or bread, have a hidden message that if you are going to all this trouble, you might as well invite someone to share it.

I have shelves of food books – more than a hundred and fifty of them – ranging from a set of cards on Indian cooking to what is called "The most sumptuous book on entertaining ever published". Some try to be comprehensive, while others like "French Provincial Cuisine", are quite specific. Even the booklets that come with the pressure cooker or food processor assume you are looking for something new.

Before you can plan a feast, you need to be confident about everyday food. Providing daily meals can be seen as a disagreeable necessity, like taking medicine. Or, you can regard it as a hobby and spend odd, spare moments indulging it. Like bridge, jigsaw puzzles or exercise, the more you do, the more fascinated you become. So I'm not ashamed to say that the idea for this book was to persuade you to come into the kitchen and then make you want to stay there.

Yet finding the time is always a problem, and never more so than for a party. The process starts with making decisions: the time and date, the number of people and, depending on these three, the menu. Always in the background is the nagging thought that there will never be enough time to do the cooking. Assuming that you have other things that take up your working day, the answer to this dilemma is to cook in stages.

Getting ahead is not a new idea. Advice for Christmas is usually to make a countdown plan. The pudding should be made in January, the presents can be bought in the July sales. That leaves the last two weeks of December for detailed notes on how to stuff the sprouts and what to do when you find that the turkey won't fit inside the oven. Yet having a deadline makes everything worse. It would be better if you could approach the idea of entertaining from another direction: choose the type of food you are good at making and then plan who to invite and when.

My leather-bound dinner books include dozens of parties and most of them could have been better; maybe not for the guests, who are on the eating side, but for me, on the worrying, planning and cooking side. What makes me nervous is a list of real or imaginary problems: Will I get it all done in time? Is the main course getting spoilt? Will there be enough? What if the guests don't turn up?

The notes I wrote were often brief. –"Terrible evening. I fell asleep at dinner." –"Hurriedly prepared meal as Carmen the au pair came and left." –"Needed more wine. One glass each wasn't enough." How could I have been so mean? I remember now, it was a 10th birthday party and the drink in question was non-alcoholic peach wine.

All these occasions were ordinary one-off meals. When it came to organising a whole weekend, the scale was quite different. For each of our sons we planned several parties to mark their thirteenth birthday – which in Judaism has special significance. For the boy a barmitzvah is often the culmination of months of study. For the parents it's a chance to invite everyone to a celebration.

For the first one, the preparations began months in advance. I had filled the enormous chest freezer in Hatch End with pastries, petit fours, stuffed chickens and whole salmons. With hopeless timing, a few weeks before the great day, we moved house. The removal van arrived but I remember nothing about packing the china or getting the furniture through the doors. Instead I have a vivid picture of explaining to the removal men that they would get their cup of tea as soon as they plugged the freezer in at the other end.

Even entertaining on a small scale can seem like a mountainous task if you're not used to it. It may seem obvious but when you're arranging a party the first thing to do is to decide on the guests. It's tempting to invite people you feel guilty about but for a first try it'll be much more relaxing if you choose very good friends. Returning hospitality and inviting the boss can come later.

Next, the drinks. More important than serving the right wine for every course is having enough to drink. As well as providing alcohol you need to cater for everyone who is driving and/or very thirsty by offering plenty of juice or fizzy water. Bottles of still mineral water are good for those who don't trust tap water (though there is a theory that nearly everyone who serves it, does so because they think other people prefer it.) The 'correct' drink to serve before a meal need not be whisky or gin. It's a lot easier to buy recommended wines from a good supermarket and just start serving a chilled bottle when people arrive. The whole point of a drink is to make everyone – including you – feel at ease, though as this tale shows, it can have the reverse effect.

A young journalist once went to interview a best selling author. The nervous young man was invited into a penthouse living-room and offered a glass of champagne – at eleven o'clock in the morning. Accepting nervously, the journalist balanced the drink and his tape-recorder while the author reached for a mug of coffee, saying "I never drink champagne at this time of day."

Having decided on the guests and the drinks, you can now put your mind to the food. The feast menu can be a lunch for four, dinner for six, brunch for ten or a buffet for twelve. If you're very confident, or you have help, you can multiply the numbers but not many people in their right mind would consider making a hot meal for a large crowd.

Once you have issued the invitations, you can concentrate on the two main concerns about the food. Is it going to taste good and is there going to be enough? Even if you've only succeeded with a fraction of the recipes so far, there will still be a dozen things you can do well. If you like to try out new ideas, don't risk it on the day, but go for the ones which can be frozen or made the day before, because if anything goes wrong, you'll know in good time. To make sure about the quantities, it's usually better to offer too much, though you needn't expect everyone to eat a full portion of everything you make.

The amazing Martha Stewart, the American writer, is clearly an expert at entertaining. She copes with midnight omelette suppers for thirty and serves a whole sucking pig with a necklace of star fruit for a Hawaiian luau. For her, getting ahead means serious planning. To organise a clambake for forty friends she starts with a map to find a suitable beach and then works out the tides. I am impressed with her catering and her style. Yet I am delighted, as you will be, that even she has a confession to make. "In the awkward moments before a party begins, authorities say you should be relaxed and enjoying a drink and I am not".

One thing is sure – the less you have to do when the guests arrive, the happier you will be. So there are no countdowns here listing what you should be doing three hours, one hour or half an hour before lift off. However, you might spend time getting friendly with the neighbours so that you can borrow space in their fridge or freezer. It's also a good idea to do all the shopping in advance, so you don't have to dash out for an egg in the middle of baking. It's even better if you can persuade someone else to shop while you get on with the cooking.

Why not start by writing a list of the things you fancy making and then decide who you're going to invite to share them? For extra peace of mind it's not a bad idea to get half the food stashed away and then pick up the phone.

Smoked Salmon Rolls

You can buy similar little appetisers but they are expensive. If you need a lot, it is cheaper to make them at home — this amount makes about 20. Cutting the smoked salmon into even strips will leave you with some trimmings — a great sandwich filling in between buttered granary bread.

8 oz	225g	smoked salmon
For the filling:		
2 fillets		smoked mackerel
3 tbsp		smatana or crème fraîche
		pepper (no salt)
		fresh dill for decoration

You will need: a fork or a blender.

First make the filling. Remove the skin from the mackerel and blend or mash it very well with the smatana and a little pepper. Check to see that there are no bones in the mixture.

Lay out the smoked salmon and cut it into strips about 1" (2.5cm) wide and 3" (8cm) long. Put a teaspoonful of the smoked mackerel filling at one end of a strip. Roll it away from you, holding it with one hand and smoothing out the sides with a knife to make sure the filling isn't oozing out.

Arrange the smoked salmon rolls on a large dish and keep them covered in the fridge until you are ready to serve them. At the last moment decorate with a few wisps of fresh dill. To freeze: arrange the rolls in a single layer and wrap them carefully. To defrost, put them on a plate and leave for an hour or so.

Gravlax with Senapsauce

'Buried' salmon or 'gravad-lax' was the Swedish way of preserving fish in the snow. Like smoked salmon, it is good with buttered brown bread, and is far easier than the owners of expensive delis would have you believe. It needs no cooking and takes only minutes to prepare. It does need some planning because it must be left for two days in the fridge (or snow!).

2 lbs	900g	salmon fillet with the skin left on, but no bone
I oz	25g	sugar
I oz	25g	coarse salt
15		peppercorns
a large bunch		fresh dill (some for the sauce and decoration)
For the senapsauce:		
3 tbsp		wine vinegar
I tbsp		sugar
I½ tbsp		continental mustard
4 fl oz	120ml	oil

You will need: a small bowl; a pestle and mortar or a rolling pin; greaseproof paper; clingfilm and a whisk.

Crush the peppercorns roughly. To do this, use a pestle and mortar or put them in a paper bag and press down with a rolling pin.

Mix together the sugar, salt and crushed pepper and sprinkle the mixture over the fish and cover it with plenty of fresh dill*. (Don't try to use dried dill because it won't taste right.) Wrap the fish first in paper and then in a double thickness of non-pvc cling film. Leave the fish in the coldest part of the fridge for two days turning it over occasionally.

For the senapsauce: Mix together the vinegar, sugar and mustard. Chop a few sprigs of dill and stir it in. Then slowly trickle in the oil, whisking with a fork until the sauce begins to thicken. Take care not to pour it too fast. The combination of oil and mustard makes an emulsion, so the technique is the same as for mayonnaise.

To serve the gravlax: Scrape off the dill mixture and cut the fish downwards with a sharp knife. The slices should be about quarter of an inch thick and not wafer thin like smoked salmon. Arrange the gravlax with sprigs of fresh dill on individual plates or a large platter.

*To keep the remaining dill fresh in the fridge: Hold open a large clear plastic bag. Put in the herbs with a few drops of water and seal the bag tightly at the top, keeping in as much air as possible.

Leek and Cheese Soufflé Pancakes

Not many hot dishes work perfectly straight from the freezer. Here is one that does. The pancakes can be filled and frozen in advance and kept in puffy refrigeration until the minute they go into the oven.

10		pancakes, using batter on page 42
For the soufflé filling:		
12 oz	350g	leeks (about 3 large ones)
½ tsp		vegetable stock cube or powder
2 oz	50g	butter and a spoonful for greasing the tins
2 oz	50g	flour
8 fl oz	225ml	milk
pinch each		paprika, pepper
6 oz	175g	gruyère cheese
4		eggs
2 oz	50g	parmesan cheese

You will need: the equipment for making the pancakes, see page 42; a shallow dish with a lid and a bowl (for the microwave) or a saucepan; a large bowl; a grater; an electric whisk; 2 large baking tins and foil or clingfilm.

First make the pancakes. For the cheese and vegetable filling, slice the leeks, using mostly the white part and wash them very well. Drain off the water, sprinkle over the vegetable stock powder and about 4 tablespoons of water, cover and microwave on **high** for 5 - 6 minutes. They should be just tender but not totally mushy. Alternatively steam them in a saucepan in a little boiling water. Drain the leeks well. Grate the cheeses on to a large plate.

For the soufflé, please refer again to the instructions on page 78. Make a thick sauce with the butter, flour and milk. Separate the eggs and add three yolks to the mixture (save the fourth for something else). Stir the sauce till it is smooth and then add the gruyère cheese, half the grated parmesan. the paprika and the pepper. (You don't need salt because the leeks and the cheese are salty enough.) Stir in the cooked leeks and leave to cool for about ten minutes.

Incidentally, if you add cheese to a sauce and continue cooking it on the hob, it will be fine. In the microwave, cooking the cheese in the sauce makes it go stringy, so it should always be added later.

Whisk the four egg whites until they are stiff and gradually fold them into the sauce.

Arrange the cooked pancakes on the worksurface and using a large spoon, pile some of the soufflé mixture into the centre of each one.

Fold over both sides so that the soufflé is completely covered and sprinkle over the rest of the parmesan. Grease the baking tins with a little butter and arrange the filled pancakes on the tins leaving some space in between them. Put them uncovered in the freezer until they harden and then cover them completely with foil or clingfilm. *Preheat the oven to 400F, 200C, Gas 6.*

To cook the frozen pancakes, put the trays into the hot oven and bake for 20 minutes. They will puff up inside and the cheese on top will have melted. If you like them crisp and brown add an extra five minutes.

Tomato Sauce

This is a basic sauce to serve with spaghetti but it is also good with the pancakes. It freezes well so it is worth making a large quantity.

2	large Spanish onions
2 tbsp	oil
2 cloves	garlic
2 large tins (800g size)	plum tomatoes
4 tbsp	tomato purée
½ tsp	dried oregano
	salt, pepper, sugar

You will need: a non-stick frying pan (optional); a large saucepan; a liquidizer or food processor or a potato masher.

Peel the onions and chop them very finely. Peel and crush the garlic cloves. In the frying pan, sauté the onions over high heat in the oil and when they start to brown add the garlic. Transfer them to the saucepan, stir well and then add the tomatoes, mashing them down with the juice and the tomato purée. Season generously with salt and black pepper and add a little sugar to taste. Sprinkle over the oregano and bring the sauce to the boil. Turn the heat down, keep the pan covered and simmer for about 30 minutes, stirring occasionally. (The point of using two pans is to prevent the sauce from sticking to the saucepan.)

For spaghetti you may prefer a chunky sauce but to serve with pancakes it is better to put the sauce into a blender and process it until it is smooth, or simply mash it to get rid of the big pieces of tomato.

To freeze: Store the cooled sauce in small, covered pots. You can defrost the sauce in a pan over gentle heat or in a microwave for a few minutes.

Tabbouleh

The bulghur or cracked wheat for this salad is uncooked. Since it has to absorb the liquid from the dressing and the vegetables, it's a perfect dish to prepare the day before. What looks like a small amount of grains makes a large bowl.

1 cup		bulghur
6 inch	15cm	piece of cucumber
2		tomatoes
3 or 4		spring onions
2 tbsp		fresh mint
4 tbsp		fresh parsley
3 fl oz	75ml	olive oil
2 tbsp		lemon juice
		salt, pepper

You will need: a bowl and a sieve.

Soak the bulghur in water for about half an hour and then drain it through a fine sieve. Peel and dice the cucumber. Cover the tomatoes with boiling water and then remove the skins. Chop the flesh into small pieces, discarding the seeds. Slice the spring onions and chop the herbs finely. Put the bulghur, cucumber and tomatoes into the bowl and then mix in the spring onion, herbs, olive oil, lemon juice and plenty of seasoning. Mix everything together very well, cover with clingfilm and refrigerate for several hours or overnight.

Raspberry and Strawberry Pavlova Roulade

Cream filled meringues which start crisp go soft after an hour or so. A pavlova is different — the inside is meant to be soft. Shaping it in a roulade keeps the berries and whipped cream enclosed so it will keep for as long as 24 hours without spoiling. This one will cut into about eight large slices.

For the meringue:

4		egg whites
6 oz	175g	sugar
2 tsp		cornflour or potato flour
1-2 tbsp		oil

For the filling:

½ pt	300ml	whipping cream
6 oz	175g	raspberries
6 oz	175g	strawberries

You will need: a swiss roll tin (a shallow tin about 10 × 8"/25cm × 20cm); 3 or 4 slightly larger sheets of greaseproof paper; a bowl and an electric whisk. Preheat the oven to 325F, 160C, Gas 3.

Sift the sugar and cornflour together to make sure there are no lumps. Whisk the egg whites until they are stiff and then slowly pour in the sugar, whisking all the time until the mixture is so firm that it won't fall out if you turn the bowl upside down.

Pour the oil on to the tin, press one of the sheets of paper over it, sliding it around to make sure that the underside is covered with the oil. Then turn it over so that the greased side is uppermost. Spoon the meringue mixture over the paper, spreading it out evenly.

Bake the pavlova for about 35 - 40 minutes. The top should be light brown and crisp. The next steps need to be done quickly before it cools. Turn the meringue over on to a clean sheet of greaseproof paper with the crisp side down. Peel off the original paper and replace it with a fresh sheet. Then roll the pavlova away from you, enclosing the paper until it forms a slightly cracked and fat swiss roll shape. Leave it to get quite cold, making sure it does not unroll.

Wash and dry the berries then whisk the cream until it is thick. Carefully unwrap the pavlova, removing the inside paper. Spread the cream over the inside of the meringue and spoon over the raspberries and strawberries. Roll up the pavlova again and lift it carefully, removing the outside paper, on to a long serving dish. Cover gently with clingfilm and refrigerate overnight. To serve it, cut it downwards into thick slices, taking care to wipe the knife each time.

Red Fruit Salad

Cut fruit usually deteriorates quickly but the juices from lightly cooked mixed berries make a brilliant red coating. This is a quick way of making fruit salad for a crowd. This amount is enough for about eight, so simply increase the quantities and cooking time if you need more.

8 oz	225g	raspberries, blackberries, red or blackcurrants
8		ripe plums
8		ripe apricots
2 - 4 tbsps		sugar
8 oz	225g	seedless grapes
To serve:		
4 oz	125g	strawberries (optional)

You will need: a large bowl; a shallow dish with a cover for the microwave or a saucepan, and clingfilm.

Mix the washed berries with two tablespoons of sugar. Stone the plums and apricots and cut them into pieces, putting half of them into the bowl. Keep it tightly covered with clingfilm. Cook the rest in a shallow dish with the berries until the fruit is just beginning to soften and the juices are starting to run. In the microwave this will take a minute or two on **high**. Or, use a saucepan and cook over low heat with about 2 fl oz water. In both cases the cooking time depends on how ripe the fruit is, but the idea is simply to release the juices, not to wait until the fruit has turned mushy.

Taste for sweetness, adding a little more sugar if you like. When the cooked fruit is cool, fold it, with the grapes, into the uncooked fruit in the bowl, coating it with the red juice. Cover and chill in the fridge overnight.

To serve: If you have any extra berries, arrange them on the top or slice them up and stir them into the fruit salad.

Kumquat Preserve

This will keep for a few days in the fridge, or can be frozen. It goes very well with duck.

4 oz	125g	kumquats
2 tsp		sugar

You will need: a shallow bowl for the microwave or a small saucepan.

Cut the kumquats in half, lengthwise, and take out any pips you can see. Arrange the fruit in a shallow container, sprinkle over the sugar and a tablespoon of water. Cover and cook on **high** for 3 – 4 minutes. The kumquats should soften and wrinkle slightly. Spoon them into a small pot, removing any pips, and leave to cool.

Alternatively, cook the fruit with the sugar and three or four tablespoons of water in a pan, and simmer over low heat, until most of the water has evaporated and the kumquats are soft.

Plum Sauce

A slightly tart accompaniment to any cold meat – especially lamb. It's a great improvement on tomato ketchup.

8 oz	225g	red plums (about 4)
1 tbsp		redcurrant jelly

You will need: a shallow bowl for the microwave or a small saucepan and a strainer.

Wash the plums, cut them into small pieces and throw away the stones. Cook them gently until they soften (this will take 3 minutes on **high** in a covered dish in the microwave or some minutes more with a little added water in a pan on the hob). Stir in the redcurrant jelly and then press the plums through a strainer to make a thick purée.Lea ve to cool.

To freeze: store the puréed sauce in a covered pot. Defrost at room temperature for a couple of hours or a minute or so on **defrost** in the microwave.

Choose Your Feast

Starters

Parmesan Toasts

Smoked Salmon Rolls

Gravlax with Senapsauce

Main Courses

Leek and Cheese Soufflé Pancakes with Tomato Sauce

Rolled Stuffed Chicken with Plum Sauce

Veal with Chestnut Mushroom Sauce

Apple Stuffed Duck with Kumquat Preserve

Side Dishes

Tabbouleh

Red Cabbage with Apples

Peppers with Rice

Desserts

Raspberry and Strawberry Pavlova Roulade

Red Fruit Salad

White and Dark Chocolate Terrine

The Feast

In the gallery of Westminster Hall, an invited audience stood and watched while an extraordinary scene unfolded. The date was 1685. The occasion was the Coronation of King James II. A geometric pattern of pies and puddings covered every inch of the long tables. There was no space for serving plates or glasses: they were passed by servants standing behind the diners. Adding to the general hubbub was the clatter of hooves as men on horseback rode up and down the centre aisle. Upstairs the observers watched as the massive array of food was consumed below.

Catering for celebration parties has changed in style, though quantity is still seen by many hosts as the first necessity in entertaining. In the Middle East, weddings are an excuse for bringing out platters of stuffed vegetables, shashlik of lamb and jewelled rice. The women will have spent days in the kitchen chopping pistachio nuts for the multi-layered baklava and preparing enough meat and chicken to feed all their friends, and a hundred more.

When it comes to paying for a feast in a restaurant the customer expects quantity and quality. Chinese or Indian waiters probably have special training in arranging a dozen dishes on a tiny table for two. Yet abundance is not the aim of French chefs who offer a 'menu dégustation' in expensive country manors. Starting with an 'amuse gueule' (which could be roughly translated as a 'fun guzzle') the discerning customer will be offered a sequence of eight or ten delicate courses; perfect examples of the range of expertise on offer. The price will be high – even a copy of the menu will add an extra seven pounds to the bill, but the food will be memorable.

A night to remember occurred some years ago at the Dorchester Hotel in London. Anton Mosimann was the head chef, famed for his cuisine and his courteous behaviour to his highly-trained staff. On this occasion a famous film star had booked in to the hotel. At midnight she happened to fancy a meal. She summoned Mosimann and ordered roast beef, Yorkshire pudding, mashed potatoes and a hot dessert with Devonshire cream. At 2 am he wheeled it into her suite. Years later she described it as one of the most memorable experiences of her life. He, on the other hand, may have preferred to forget it.

The grand style normally associated with Hollywood movies can contribute to the sense of occasion that goes with great food. I've experienced it only once. The Ritz Hotel in Madrid is a stone's throw from the famous Prado museum. It is a huge old-fashioned hotel where the staff whisk away the linen towels twice a day and the bathroom is larger than most people's living rooms. There is a courtyard outside where you can sip a drink in the dappled light of the late afternoon sun under trailing vine leaves. What sets the Ritz apart is the way they serve breakfast. Expecting a run-of-the-mill room service meal, I opened my eyes at 9 am to see a waiter wheeling in one of those trolleys with expanding sides that turn into a table. He unfolded a crisply laundered white cloth and set out the breakfast. There was a large glass jug of juice made from sweet Valencia oranges. Inside a folded serviette were two croissants – crisp on the outside and warm inside. There were fresh rolls and slices of fragrant almond cake, with a bowl of cherry jam and cool, unsalted butter. On the tray were fine porcelain cups and a pot of strong, hot coffee with cream.

Analysing what made this such a great experience made me realise some of the ingredients of a true feast: the food and drink have to be better than you would expect and someone else should present it to you.

Whenever I catered a grand party I used to wonder, in the middle of all the work, why I was doing it. Most actors who have ever forgotten their lines at a dress rehearsal would know the feeling. But at the end of the show, when the audience is clapping, it's clear that it's all worth it. Preparing a successful feast and collapsing in a heap after everyone has gone home will give you the same buzz.

There's no need for hesitation – you know you can do it.

Parmesan Toasts

Although these appetisers have to be served warm, they can be prepared early in the day and the only work you need to do at the last minute is opening the oven door. This will make a dozen small rounds.

4 thin slices		white bread
½ oz	15g	butter
1 oz	25g	fresh parmesan cheese
1 oz	25g	almond flakes

You will need: a round metal biscuit cutter (2"/5cm diameter); a bun tin with 12 indentations; a pastry brush and a grater.

Cut the bread into rounds with the cutter. Soften the butter slightly (don't melt it) and brush it over the base of the bun tin. Press in the bread. Grate the cheese on to a plate and put a small spoonful on to each round. Scatter over the almonds, pressing them down slightly on top of the cheese. You can do all this in advance, but to stop them drying out, keep the tin covered if you are not going to cook them immediately .

Preheat the oven to 350F, 180C, Gas 4.

Uncover the tin and cook the rounds for 10 minutes. The bread will have toasted and the almonds will be crisp and brown. Take out the toasts and serve within the next 15 minutes.

Rolled Stuffed Chicken

An electric carving knife is useful to make neat slices of white meat with a round of sausage in the centre. If you don't have one, the problem is solved by roasting the breasts and refrigerating them overnight. They will then be firm enough to cut with an ordinary knife and will serve 8 - 12 as part of a cold buffet.

4	chicken breasts with the skin
For the stuffing:	
5 thick slices	bread without crusts
1	large onion
2 tbsp	oil
½ cup	water
	salt, pepper
8	small chipolata or frankfurter sausages

You will need: a rolling pin; some greaseproof paper; a food processor or liquidizer; a frying pan; a very sharp knife or an electric carving knife; a small baking tin and sewing cotton.

Put the chicken breasts with the skin uppermost between two sheets of paper. Flatten them slightly with the rolling pin. To make the stuffing, put the bread in the food processor or liquidizer. Buzz it up to form crumbs. Chop the onion and sauté it in the heated oil in the frying pan, stirring to make sure the pieces brown evenly. Season with salt and pepper and pour over the water which will turn brown from the onions. Bring it to the boil and then, for a few seconds, blend together the crumbs and the onion mixture. Leave the stuffing to cool. Cook the frankfurters in boiling water for a few minutes (they are already partly cooked) and leave these to cool too.
Preheat the oven to 350F, 180C, Gas 4.

Spread out the chicken breasts with the skin side down. Divide the stuffing evenly over the meat and arrange the sausages across the narrower end of each breast. Roll them up, pulling the skin round to make sure the stuffing is completely enclosed. Tie each one with a length of cotton.

Brush the baking tin with oil and put in the chicken breasts with the seam side down, so that they won't uncurl. Roast for about 45 minutes, pouring off any juices after about 20 minutes. This can be used for soup or gravy, but if the chicken is left standing in a pool of juice it will stew rather than roast.

Leave the rolls to cool on a plate and then refrigerate. When they are quite firm slice them into rounds about the width of a pencil.

Veal with Chestnut Mushroom Sauce

You can use escalopes of veal or thinly sliced breasts of turkey for this easy, hot main course for six. Boiling some small new potatoes to go with it will take about the same time.

2 lbs	900g	thin slices of veal or turkey
6 tbsp		flour
6 - 8 tbsp		oil
12		chestnut mushrooms
1 cup		fine sherry
1 cup		water
		salt, pepper

You will need: a rolling pin; greaseproof paper; a large plate; a very large frying pan and an ovenproof serving dish.

Put the slices of veal or turkey in between two sheets of paper and flatten them with the rolling pin. Season the flour with salt and pepper and toss each slice in it to coat both sides. Wipe the mushrooms and cut them into thin slices.

Heat a little oil in the frying pan and fry the mushroom slices over high heat until they are brown. Slide them on to a plate while you cook the veal. Heat some oil and over medium heat sauté half the meat for about four minutes on each side, turning it frequently to brown it slightly. You will need to fry the veal in two batches, as there will probably be too much to go into the pan in one layer.

Pile all the slices back into the frying pan and then pour over the sherry which will immediately start to sizzle. Add the water and stir the veal and the sauce over high heat to reduce it slightly. Add the cooked mushrooms and any juices, lower the heat and continue cooking for a few more minutes.

To serve: Spoon the veal and the sauce into the serving dish and keep it warm, covered, in a very low oven 250F, 130C, Gas 1/2 for up to 15 minutes but not more.

Apple Stuffed Duck

This is like the stuffed chicken, with a similar filling and method. In the centre are whole apples filled with macerated (soaked) sultanas which gives it a very pretty cross section when it is cut. It will serve four hot, but will make about 12 slices if it is left to get cold.

2		large breasts of duck with the skin
3		large onions (I for the stuffing, 2 for roasting)
2 tbsp		oil
6 oz	175g	breadcrumbs
		salt, pepper
I½ oz	40g	sultanas or raisins
I tbsp		Calvados or brandy
8		very small cox apples

You will need: a bowl; an apple corer or a thin sharp knife; a shallow dish with a cover for the microwave or a saucepan; sewing cotton; a baking tin with a rack; an electric carving knife and a strainer.

First prepare the duck breasts and, using one onion and the breadcrumbs, make the stuffing (as in the recipe on page 188). Leave it to cool while you prepare the apples.

Put the sultanas and the liqueur in a saucer and microwave on **high** for about a minute to plump up the dried fruit. Alternatively pour some boiling water over the fruit and leave for at least half an hour. Drain off the water and leave to soak in the liqueur for another 15 minutes.

Remove the cores carefully from four of the apples, taking care not to break them, then peel off the skin. (If you do it the other way the apples are more likely to split.) Peel the rest of the apples and cut them into slices. Microwave the slices on **high** for about 3 minutes when they should be cooked but not collapsed. Alternatively poach the apples in very little water until they are soft.

Preheat the oven to 425F, 220C, Gas 7.

Press the sultanas into the centre of the apples. Spread out the duck breasts, cover them with the stuffing and then arrange two apples on each. Roll them up so that you can see the sultanas at each end. Tie the rolls with a length of cotton, winding it round and underneath to make sure the stuffing and apples are secure. Prick the skin in several places.

Cut the two remaining onions into thick slices and arrange them on the base of an ungreased baking tin. Put the duck breasts, which will release a lot of fat, on top and roast for 20 minutes. Lift the tin out of the oven and carefully pour any fat and juices into a bowl. Continue roasting the duck breasts for another 20 minutes, pour off the fat again and lower the heat to 325F, 170C, Gas 3. They will now take another 40 minutes at this lower temperature and will be tender and brown.

To serve the duck hot: Slice each breast downwards, through the apples, very carefully. Each one will make about 6 thick slices. Arrange the slices on a large platter and keep them warm, covered, while you make the gravy. Pour the fatty pan juices into the bowl and then discard the fat from the top. Pour the juices which will be underneath back into the tin with the roasted onion slices. Add about two cups of water and bring to the boil on the hob, stirring in all the brown bits. Continue bubbling for a few minutes to reduce the liquid, taste for seasoning and strain the gravy into a bowl or sauceboat. Serve the duck slices with a spoonful of the onions and the cool apple slices.

To serve the duck cold: Leave the stuffed breasts to cool and when they are quite cold cut each one downwards into six or seven slices. Arrange them on a large platter and serve with Kumquat Preserve (page 183).

Red Cabbage with Apples

The colour from the cabbage turns the apples a warm pink and the dish can be served hot as a vegetable or cold as a salad. There are no instructions for conventional cooking as the 'no-water' method of keeping the colour and flavour only works in the microwave.

2		crisp eating apples
8 oz	225g	red cabbage (about half a small one)
I tbsp		hazelnut oil
		salt, pepper

You will need: a shallow covered dish for the microwave.

Peel and core the apples and cut them into chunks. Slice the red cabbage into shreds with a sharp knife and put them in the dish with the apples. Cover and shake it slightly to mix them together. Cook on **high** for 3 - 4 minutes when the apples should be just soft and the cabbage slightly wilted. Season with salt and pepper and toss in the hazelnut oil.

Peppers with Rice

You can fill the peppers early and reheat them in the oven. A quick burst in the microwave would be better and stop them drying out, but you would need to divide the 16 halves into two dishes and do one at a time.

8		red, orange and yellow peppers
8 oz	225g	raw rice (or 1 quantity cooked rice)
4 - 8 tbsp		olive oil (microwaving uses less)
3		spring onions
		small piece of ginger root
4 oz	125g	cooked chicken or salami
		salt, pepper

You will need: a non-stick frying pan; a shallow dish for the microwave and a colander or strainer.

First prepare the peppers by halving and deseeding them. Whether you are cooking them in the microwave or in a pan, you will need to do at least two batches. Cook them, covered, on **high** in the microwave, for 3 minutes. Drizzle over a tablespoon of olive oil and cook uncovered for another 2 to 3 minutes or until they are soft. Repeat with the rest of the peppers. Alternatively fry them in oil for a few minutes, turning them over frequently until they are soft. Arrange the peppers on a large dish and keep them warm.

For the filling, chop the spring onions and boil and drain the rice. Or, use cold cooked rice, as in the recipe on page 143. Heat the remaining oil in the frying pan and toss in the spring onion and almost immediately add the drained rice. Add the pieces of cooked chicken or salami, grate over some ginger root and seasoning and keep stirring for a few minutes over medium heat until the rice and chicken are hot. Spoon the filling into the halved peppers.

To serve them later: Reheat the peppers, covered, on two separate round dishes. This will take 2 to 4 minutes on **high**, depending on whether they are warm or have been refrigerated. The centre of the peppers should be piping hot and the rice will be moist.

To reheat them conventionally, put them on a large ovenproof dish, cover with foil and cook in a preheated oven (350F, 180C, Gas 4) for about fifteen minutes.

White and Dark Chocolate Terrine

This is a half-frozen, layered mousse or 'semifreddo'. Ideally it should be made about six hours before you want to serve it, when the outside will be firm and the centre will be slightly soft. If you don't have the right size tins you can make it in individual pots or glasses. It makes about 14 slices or 12 pots.

For the dark chocolate mousse:

5 oz	150g	fine dark chocolate
4		eggs
4 fl oz	115ml	whipping cream (from 10 fl oz carton)

For the white chocolate mousse:

5 oz	150g	white chocolate
4		eggs
6 fl oz	170ml	whipping cream (the rest of the carton)

For decoration:

		chocolate spirals (page 90)

You will need: 2 large baking tins (11 × 16 ×1"/28cm × 4cm × 2.5cm); 3 large bowls; an electric whisk; greaseproof paper. clingfilm and a palette knife.

If you haven't made a mousse before, please follow the instructions on page 90. This recipe is just the same, except for the addition of whipped cream.

Make one colour at a time, using the ingredients above. Melt the chocolate in the microwave on **high** for about one and a half minutes or over boiling water. Beat in the yolks and then stir in some of the whisked egg whites. Whip the cream till it is just beginning to thicken but is not too stiff and fold 4 fl oz (115ml) into the dark mousse and 6 fl oz (170ml) into the white one.

Line the tins with paper or clingfilm and spread out the mousses. Freeze for about two to three hours until they are firm. Cut each mousse into half horizontally and then, using the palette knife, pile a dark strip on top of a light one, alternating the colours again until all four are used up. Continue freezing the assembled terrine for a few more hours and then mark it into slices. If you prefer you can simply layer the two mousses in small pots or glasses and chill the dessert instead of freezing it.

To serve the terrine, take it out of the freezer after about 6 hours and serve immediately. If it has been frozen for longer, let it defrost in the fridge for about an hour but the consistency will be different. The centre will be harder and the outside will start to melt slightly. Decorate it with some frozen chocolate spirals.

Acknowledgements

There are two ways to learn how to cook – watching and reading. Before I ever attempted a single dish, I had absorbed a wealth of knowledge, sitting on a chair in my mother's kitchen.

To translate those tastes into reality I turned to books about food. In the early days I enjoyed the clarity of Marguerite Patten and Jane Grigson. Then came happy experiments with the inventive recipes of Josceline Dimbleby and Martha Stewart. The two authors whose prose made me want to rush into the kitchen were Laurie Colwen and Harold McGee. Many other chefs and writers have sown the seeds for some of the ideas I have developed. To all of them I am grateful.

This book is the culmination of many months of cooking and writing. I would like to thank Michael for his patience when there was no food on the table and for discussing the project on every occasion when there was. Daniel's advice on design has been invaluable. Finally I am grateful to Adam for many hours of work, for his skill with typography and layout and for his boundless enthusiasm.

Index